HEALTH & FIBRE
COOKERY

Edited by Norma MacMillan and Wendy James
Home Economist Gilly Cubitt

ORBIS PUBLISHING London

Introduction

Healthy ingredients such as fresh vegetables, pulses, dried and fresh fruits, yogurt, nuts, cereals, dairy products and lean meat, poultry and fish are used in this book to make delicious recipes that are good for you too!

Both imperial and metric measures are given for each recipe; you should follow only one set of measures as they are not direct conversions. All spoon measures are level unless otherwise stated. Pastry quantities are based on the amount of flour used. Dried herbs may be substituted for fresh herbs; use one-third of the quantity.

Photographs were supplied by Editions Atlas, Editions Atlas/Masson, Editions Atlas/Zadora, Archivio IGDA, Lavinia Press Agency, Orbis GmbH

The material in this book has previously appeared in *The Complete Cook*

First published 1983 in Great Britain by Orbis Publishing Limited, 20–22 Bedfordbury, London WC2

ISBN 0-85613-564-X
Printed in Italy

Contents

Soups

Chicken and corn soup

Overall timing 1½ hours

Freezing Not suitable

To serve 6

1	Large onion	1
1 oz	Vegetable margarine	25 g
2 lb	Chicken portions	900 g
¼ teasp	Ground cumin	1.25 ml
2½ pints	Chicken stock	1.5 litres
1 lb	Floury potatoes	450 g
	Salt and pepper	
2	Cobs of sweetcorn	2
1	Ripe avocado	1
¼ pint	Plain yogurt	150 ml

Peel and chop onion. Heat margarine in a large saucepan, add chicken and onion and fry for 5 minutes, turning chicken occasionally. Add cumin and fry for 2 minutes. Add stock and bring to the boil. Cover and simmer for 35 minutes till chicken is tender. Meanwhile, peel and dice potatoes.

Lift chicken out of pan. Add potatoes to stock, season and simmer for 10 minutes till tender. Meanwhile, remove skin and bones from chicken and cut flesh into strips. Wash corn, discarding husks. Cut across into 1 inch (2.5 cm) thick slices.

Mash potatoes in the soup to thicken it. Bring to the boil and add corn slices and chicken flesh. Simmer for 10 minutes.

Peel and halve avocado. Remove stone, and slice flesh thinly. Place in a tureen with yogurt. Taste soup and adjust seasoning. Pour into tureen and serve.

Thick bean soup

Overall timing 1¾ hours plus overnight soaking

Freezing Not suitable

To serve 4

7 oz	Dried kidney beans	200 g
1	Bouquet garni	1
2	Onions	2
1	Clove	1
1	Garlic clove	1
1 teasp	Salt	5 ml
2 tbsp	Vegetable margarine	2x15 ml
1 tbsp	Tomato purée	15 ml
	Black pepper	
	Beef stock cube	

Place the beans in a bowl and cover with water. Leave to soak overnight.

Drain beans and place in saucepan. Cover with fresh water, add the bouquet garni, 1 of the onions (spiked with the clove) and garlic, peeled. Bring to the boil over a medium heat and cook for 35 minutes. Add salt and continue cooking for a further 35 minutes.

Melt the margarine in frying pan. Peel and chop remaining onion and cook for a few minutes. Remove from heat, lift out onion with a draining spoon and place in blender.

Drain beans and strain cooking liquor into a measuring jug. Discard onion and clove. Put beans into blender with tomato purée, pepper and 1¾ pints/1 litre of stock (made up of cooking liquor and water plus stock cube). Blend for a few seconds, then pour into saucepan. Bring gently to the boil, then simmer for 15 minutes, stirring frequently.

Taste and adjust seasoning if necessary. Pour into tureen and serve with croûtons.

Minestrone with pumpkin

Overall timing 35 minutes

Freezing Not suitable

To serve 6

1 lb	Pumpkin	450 g
2	Medium-size potatoes	2
8 oz	Small turnips	225 g
2 oz	Vegetable margarine	50 g
1 pint	Milk	600 ml
1½ pints	Chicken stock	900 ml
	Salt and pepper	
2 oz	Wholemeal spaghetti	50 g
6	Spinach or beetroot leaves	6

Scrape the seeds and fibrous centre out of the pumpkin. Remove the skin and cut the flesh into chunks. Peel the potatoes and turnips and cut into chunks.

Heat the margarine in a flameproof casserole, add the vegetables, cover and sweat over a low heat for 5 minutes. Stir in the milk and stock, season and bring to the boil. Simmer for 10 minutes.

Break the spaghetti into convenient lengths. Wash and shred the spinach or beetroot leaves and add to the soup with the spaghetti. Simmer for a further 10–15 minutes till pasta is al dente.

Adjust the seasoning and serve immediately with crusty bread.

Veal and sauerkraut soup

Overall timing 1 hour 50 minutes plus soaking

Freezing Not suitable

To serve 4–6

3 oz	Dried borlotti beans	75 g
4 oz	Smoked streaky bacon rashers	100 g
1	Large onion	1
2	Garlic cloves	2
2 tbsp	Vegetable oil	2 x 15 ml
8 oz	Lean minced veal	225 g
	Salt	
2 tbsp	Chopped parsley	2 x 15 ml
4 teasp	Plain wholemeal flour	4 x 5 ml
8 oz	Sauerkraut	225 g

Rinse the beans and put into a saucepan with 1¾ pints (1 litre) of boiling water. Bring to the boil and boil for 2 minutes. Remove from the heat, cover and leave to soak for 2 hours.

Derind and dice the bacon. Peel the onion and garlic and chop finely. Heat the oil in a frying pan, add the minced veal and fry till browned all over. Add ½ teasp (2.5 ml) salt, the bacon, onion, garlic and parsley. Fry for 5 minutes, then add flour and cook, stirring, for a further 5 minutes.

Add mixture to beans. Bring to the boil, stirring, then cover and simmer for 1 hour till beans are tender but not mushy.

Stir sauerkraut into mixture and cook for a further 15 minutes. Taste and adjust the seasoning, pour into a warmed tureen and serve immediately.

Radish top soup

Overall timing 45 minutes

Freezing Suitable

To serve 4–6

2	Bunches of radish tops	2
2	Onions	2
2	Large floury potatoes	2
2 oz	Vegetable margarine	50 g
2½ pints	Chicken stock	1.5 litres
2	Thick slices of wholemeal bread	2
2 tbsp	Vegetable oil	2 x 15 ml
	Salt and pepper	

Wash, trim and thoroughly drain the radish tops. Peel and chop the onions; peel and dice the potatoes. Heat half the margarine in a saucepan, add the onions and potatoes and fry for 5 minutes without browning. Add the radish tops and cook, stirring, for 3 minutes. Add stock and simmer for about 10 minutes till the potatoes are tender.

Meanwhile, cut the bread into small cubes. Heat the remaining margarine and the oil in a frying pan and fry the bread, turning frequently, till golden. Drain on kitchen paper.

Purée the soup in a blender or rub through a sieve. Return to the saucepan and heat through. Taste and adjust the seasoning, then pour into a warmed soup tureen. Scatter the croûtons over and serve immediately.

Bean soup

Overall timing 30 minutes

Freezing Suitable: add yogurt after thawing

To serve 4

4 oz	Streaky bacon	125 g
1	Red pepper	1
1	Green pepper	1
1¾ pints	Strong beef stock	1 litre
12 oz	Can of butter beans	340 g
	Tabasco sauce	
	Salt	
4 tbsp	Plain yogurt	4 x 15 ml

Derind and chop bacon and fry it lightly in a frying pan till the fat runs. Place in a deep saucepan.

Deseed and finely chop half the red and green peppers and add to the pan with the stock (made up with 3 stock cubes if necessary) and drained beans. Bring to the boil and simmer for 20 minutes.

Add Tabasco sauce and salt to taste.

Slice remaining peppers and blanch for 5 minutes in boiling water. Drain well.

Remove soup from the heat and stir in the yogurt. Garnish with pepper slices and serve with a bowl of grated cheese and fresh wholemeal bread.

Vegetable soup

Overall timing 1 hour

Freezing Suitable

To serve 6

2	Large onions	2
1	Large leek	1
2 oz	Vegetable margarine	50 g
1	Garlic clove	1
8 oz	Ripe tomatoes	225 g
$1\frac{1}{2}$ lb	White cabbage	700 g
$2\frac{1}{2}$ pints	Water	1.5 litres
1	Bay leaf	1
	Salt and pepper	
1	Red pepper	1
1 tbsp	Chopped fresh dill	15 ml

Peel and chop the onion. Wash and trim the leek, cut into 1 inch (2.5 cm) lengths, then into quarters. Heat the margarine in a large saucepan, add the onions and leek and fry, stirring, for about 10 minutes till golden.

Peel and crush the garlic. Add to pan. Blanch, peel and finely chop tomatoes; wash and shred the cabbage. Add to the pan and fry for 3 minutes, stirring well to release any sediment. Stir in the water, add bay leaf and bring to the boil. Season, cover and simmer for 20 minutes.

Meanwhile, wash, deseed and thinly slice the pepper. Add to the soup and simmer for a further 10 minutes. Remove from the heat, stir in the dill and adjust the seasoning. Serve immediately with wholemeal or rye bread.

Iced cucumber soup

Overall timing 15 minutes plus chilling

Freezing Not suitable

To serve 6

$\frac{1}{2}$ pint	Plain yogurt	300 ml
1 pint	Milk	560 ml
$\frac{1}{4}$ pint	Dry white wine	150 ml
1 tbsp	Lemon juice	15 ml
1	Small onion	1
2	Garlic cloves	2
	Salt and pepper	
	Sugar	
1	Large cucumber	1
	Cress or sprigs of mint	

Whisk yogurt and milk together in a bowl. Add wine and lemon juice, whisking all the time. Peel the onion, then finely grate it into mixture. Peel and crush the garlic and add. Season well with salt, pepper and a pinch of sugar.

Wash and dry cucumber. Cut off a few slices and reserve for garnish. Grate the rest (remove skin first if preferred) and add to yogurt mixture with a little finely chopped cress and mint. Alternatively, place all ingredients in a blender and purée until smooth.

Chill for 1 hour. Garnish with reserved cucumber slices and cress or mint.

Barley and celery soup

Overall timing $2\frac{1}{2}$ hours

Freezing Suitable: add egg yolks, cream and remaining butter after thawing in a double boiler

To serve 4–6

8 oz	Pearl barley	225 g
2 oz	Vegetable margarine	50 g
$1\frac{3}{4}$ pints	Water	1 litre
$1\frac{3}{4}$ pints	Chicken stock	1 litre
	Salt and pepper	
4	Stalks of celery	4
2	Egg yolks	2
$\frac{1}{4}$ pint	Plain yogurt	150 ml

Wash the barley under running water and drain well. Melt half the margarine in a saucepan. Add barley and brown lightly, stirring with a wooden spoon. Pour in hot water and stock. Bring to the boil and season with salt and pepper. Cover, reduce heat and cook gently for about $1\frac{1}{4}$ hours.

Chop the celery, and add to the pan. Cook for 1 hour more.

Lightly whisk egg yolks and yogurt and pour into a warmed soup tureen. Cut remaining margarine into small pieces and stir into tureen. Pour in soup, season with pepper, whisk lightly and serve immediately.

Hungarian cabbage soup

Overall timing 2 hours

Freezing Suitable: add flour and yogurt when reheating

To serve 4

8 oz	Onions	225 g
1	Garlic clove	1
3 tbsp	Vegetable oil	3x15 ml
12 oz	Stewing beef	350 g
12 oz	Canned sauerkraut	350 g
$\frac{1}{2}$ teasp	Fennel seeds	2.5 ml
$\frac{1}{2}$ teasp	Coarse salt	2.5 ml
$3\frac{1}{2}$ pints	Stock	2 litres
4 oz	Streaky bacon	125 g
2	Frankfurters	2
1 tbsp	Paprika	15 ml
2 tbsp	Plain wholemeal flour	2x15 ml
4 tbsp	Water	4x15 ml
2 tbsp	Plain yogurt	2x15 ml

Peel and slice onions; peel and crush garlic. Heat 2 tbsp (2x15 ml) oil in large saucepan. Add onions and garlic and fry over moderate heat till golden. Cut beef into small cubes, add to pan and brown all over.

Add drained canned sauerkraut, fennel seeds and coarse salt to the pan. Cover with the stock (made with 2 stock cubes if necessary) and simmer gently for 1 hour or till meat is tender.

Derind and roughly chop the bacon. Fry bacon in remaining oil in a frying pan till crisp, then add the sliced frankfurters and paprika. Cook for 5 minutes, then remove and add to the saucepan.

Blend flour with cold water in a bowl till smooth, then stir into the soup mixture and cook for a further 5 minutes. Stir in the yogurt, adjust the seasoning and serve at once with slices of black bread.

Grapefruit cocktails

Overall timing 10 minutes plus chilling

Freezing Not suitable

To serve 4

1	Grapefruit	1
1	Clementine	1
1	Orange	1
1	Apple	1
1	Pear	1
2 tbsp	Lemon juice	2x15ml
2 tbsp	Vodka (optional)	2x15ml
	Salt and pepper	
	Lettuce leaves	
6 tbsp	Plain yogurt	6x15ml

Peel grapefruit, clementine and orange. Remove pips. Core apple and pear. Chop fruit and place in a bowl. Sprinkle with lemon juice and vodka, if used. Season lightly and chill for 2 hours.

Wash and dry lettuce leaves. Arrange in individual serving dishes. Carefully stir yogurt into chilled fruit mixture. Divide between dishes and serve.

Esau's salad

Overall timing 1 hour plus cooling

Freezing Not suitable

To serve 6

1 lb	Continental lentils	450 g
2 oz	Smoked bacon	50 g
4 tbsp	Oil	4x15 ml
2	Frankfurters	2
1 tbsp	Vinegar	15 ml
1 teasp	Made mustard	5 ml
	Salt and pepper	
1	Onion	1
1	Green pepper	1
2	Tomatoes	2
2	Hard-boiled eggs	2
1 tbsp	Chopped parsley or chives	15 ml

Put lentils in a saucepan and add enough water just to cover. Bring to the boil, cover and simmer for about 1 hour till tender. Drain and leave to cool.

Derind bacon and cut into strips. Heat 1 tbsp (15 ml) of the oil in a frying pan, add bacon and cook until golden. Remove from pan and allow to cool.

Put frankfurters in a pan, cover with water and bring to the boil. Drain and leave to cool.

Meanwhile, beat together the rest of the oil, the vinegar, mustard and seasoning in a serving dish.

Peel and slice onion. Deseed and slice pepper. Put cooled lentils, bacon, onion and pepper into the dish with the dressing and mix well.

Cut tomatoes into wedges. Shell eggs and cut into wedges. Slice frankfurters. Arrange on top of lentil salad and sprinkle with parsley or chives. Serve with black bread.

Mussels florentine

Overall timing 40 minutes

Freezing Not suitable

To serve 4

8 oz	Frozen spinach	225 g
2 pints	Mussels	1.1 litres
5 tbsp	Dry white wine	5x15 ml
1 oz	Vegetable margarine	25 g
1 oz	Plain wholemeal flour	25 g
$\frac{1}{4}$ pint	Milk	150 ml
4 oz	Grated cheese	125 g
4 tbsp	Plain yogurt	4x15 ml
	Salt and pepper	
3 tbsp	Vegetable oil	3x15 ml
8	Thick slices of wholemeal bread	8

Unwrap spinach, place in a sieve and leave to thaw. Scrub and wash the mussels. Put into a saucepan with the white wine and cook over a high heat till the shells open. Discard any that remain closed. Remove the mussels from their shells and reserve. Discard shells. Strain the cooking liquor through a muslin-lined sieve and reserve.

Preheat the oven to 400°F (200°C) Gas 6. Melt the margarine in a saucepan, add the flour and cook for 1 minute. Gradually add the milk and the reserved cooking liquor and bring to the boil, stirring constantly. Remove from heat and stir in the grated cheese and the yogurt. Season to taste.

Heat the oil in a frying pan and fry the slices of bread till golden on both sides. Arrange on a baking tray. Press the spinach till thoroughly drained and spread over the bread. Season. Divide the mussels between the slices and spoon the sauce over. Bake in the centre of the oven for 10–15 minutes till golden. Serve immediately with a tomato and onion salad.

Apple and salami salad

Overall timing 40 minutes

Freezing Not suitable

To serve 4

3	Small onions	3
3	Apples	3
8 oz	Salami	225 g
2	Large gherkins	2
1 tbsp	Vinegar	15 ml
1 tbsp	Lemon juice	15 ml
3 tbsp	Vegetable oil	3x15 ml
	Salt and pepper	
	Pinch of muscovado sugar	
$\frac{1}{4}$ teasp	Celery or mustard seeds	1.25 ml

Peel onions and cut into thin rings. Core and chop apples. Dice salami and gherkins. Put them all in a salad bowl and mix well together.

Combine all remaining ingredients to make the dressing and pour over salad, mixing it in well. Leave for 20 minutes to blend the flavours before serving, with crusty bread and butter.

Smoked mackerel hors d'oeuvre

Overall timing 15 minutes

Freezing Not suitable

To serve 4

4	Hard-boiled eggs	4
12 oz	Smoked mackerel fillets	350 g
2	Large spring onions	2
2 tbsp	Vegetable oil	2 x 15 ml
	Salt and pepper	
2 oz	Vegetable margarine	50 g
	Round wholemeal toasts	

Shell eggs and chop whites and yolks separately. Remove skin and bones from mackerel fillets and arrange to form a star on a serving dish.

Trim and wash spring onions and thinly slice the white parts. Arrange onions, chopped whites and yolks alternately between fillets. Sprinkle oil over and season. Make margarine curls and place in the centre. Halve toasts and arrange around the edge.

Vegetable terrine

Overall timing 2½ hours plus overnight soaking and chilling

Freezing Suitable: omit the hard-boiled eggs and garnish after thawing

To serve 10–12

8 oz	Dried haricot beans	225 g
2	Onions	2
3	Cloves	3
11 oz	Fresh wholemeal breadcrumbs	300 g
¼ pint	Milk	150 ml
12 oz	Carrots	350 g
4 oz	Courgettes	125 g
4 oz	Green beans	125 g
4 oz	Fresh shelled peas	125 g
10	Spring onions	10
6	Hard-boiled eggs	6
4 tbsp	Chopped herbs	4 x 15 ml
2	Eggs	2
	Salt and pepper	
1 teasp	Ground allspice	5 ml
½ pint	Thick mayonnaise	300 ml

Soak beans overnight; drain. Peel one onion and spike with cloves. Add to beans, cover with water and simmer for 1 hour.

Meanwhile, soak crumbs in milk. Chop carrots, courgettes and beans. Cook vegetables including peas till tender. Drain.

Peel and chop remaining onion. Chop spring onions; shell and chop four hard-boiled eggs. Mix all with breadcrumbs and half herbs.

Preheat the oven to 375°F (190°C) Gas 5. Drain beans. Remove cloves from onion. Purée beans, cooked onion and half vegetables. Beat in crumb mixture, eggs, seasoning, allspice and rest of vegetables. Press into greased and lined 3 pint (1.7 litre) tin and cover. Place in a roasting tin containing hot water and bake for 1 hour. Cool, then chill till firm.

Turn out terrine and garnish with rest of eggs and half mayonnaise (made with vegetable oil). Mix remainder with herbs for sauce.

Russian avocados

Overall timing 15 minutes plus marination

Freezing Not suitable

To serve 6

5 tbsp	Vegetable oil	5x15ml
2 tbsp	Wine vinegar	2x15ml
1	Garlic clove	1
	Salt and pepper	
1	Cooked potato	1
3	Cooked carrots	3
1	Cooked beetroot	1
3 tbsp	Cooked peas	3x15ml
10oz	Can of asparagus tips	280g
3	Avocados	3
2 tbsp	Lemon juice	2x15ml
6 tbsp	Plain yogurt	6x15ml
2	Hard-boiled eggs	2

To make a vinaigrette, put the oil, vinegar, peeled and crushed garlic, salt and pepper into a mixing bowl and beat with a fork until well blended.

Dice the potato, carrots and beetroot and put in a bowl with the peas and drained asparagus tips. Pour the vinaigrette over and leave to marinate for 30 minutes, stirring gently from time to time.

Cut the avocados in half lengthways. Remove stones and a little of the flesh. Chop flesh and mix in with other vegetables. Sprinkle avocado halves with lemon juice.

Fill avocado shells with vegetable mixture and top with yogurt. Chop hard-boiled eggs and sprinkle over yogurt.

Waldorf apples

Overall timing 20 minutes plus chilling

Freezing Not suitable

To serve 6

4	Stalks of celery	4
3	Dessert apples	3
1 tbsp	Lemon juice	15ml
3 tbsp	Plain yogurt	3x15ml
3 tbsp	Mayonnaise	3x15ml
	Tabasco sauce	
	Salt and pepper	
12	Small tomatoes	12
	Chopped walnuts	

Wash, trim and finely chop the celery. Peel, core and dice the apples. Sprinkle with lemon juice to prevent discoloration, then mix with the celery. Add the yogurt, mayonnaise, a few drops of Tabasco and seasoning and fold gently together.

Cut a slice from the top of each tomato and scoop out the insides with a teaspoon. Fill the tomato cases with the celery mixture. Cover and chill for 30 minutes.

Sprinkle with walnuts before serving.

Piquant herby tomatoes

Overall timing 25–30 minutes

Freezing Not suitable

To serve 4

8	Medium tomatoes	8
1	Onion	1
1 oz	Vegetable magarine	25 g
4 oz	Fresh wholemeal breadcrumbs	100 g
2 tbsp	Chopped capers	2x15 ml
2 tbsp	Chopped mixed fresh herbs	2x15 ml
1	Garlic clove	1
1	Egg	1
	Salt and pepper	
2 tbsp	Vegetable oil	2x15 ml
	Bran (optional)	

Preheat the oven to 400°F (200°C) Gas 6. Cut a slice from the top of each tomato and scoop out the insides with a teaspoon. Arrange in an oiled ovenproof dish.

Peel and finely chop the onion. Fry in the margarine until softened, then mix in the breadcrumbs, capers, herbs, garlic, egg and seasoning. Use to stuff the tomatoes. Sprinkle with bran, if using.

Pour the oil over the tomatoes. Bake for 15–20 minutes, and serve hot.

Stuffed artichokes

Overall timing 1½ hours

Freezing Not suitable

To serve 8

8	Globe artichokes	8
	Lemon juice	
4 oz	Cooked ham	100 g
4 oz	Grated cheese	100 g
1 oz	Fresh wholemeal breadcrumbs	25 g
1	Egg yolk	1
	Chopped parsley	
	Salt and pepper	
½ pint	Chicken stock	300 ml

Preheat the oven to 350°F (180°C) Gas 4. Cut the stalks and tips from the artichokes with a sharp knife. Trim the tips from the remaining leaves with kitchen scissors. Open out the leaves and scoop out the hairy choke with a teaspoon. Rinse well, then rub all cut surfaces with lemon juice.

Dice the ham and mix well with the cheese, breadcrumbs, egg yolk, parsley and seasoning. Stuff into the centres of the artichokes.

Arrange in an oiled baking dish and pour around the stock. Cover and bake for 1 hour, basting with the stock from time to time. Serve hot.

Trout with sorrel sauce

Overall timing 40 minutes

Freezing Not suitable

To serve 4

8 oz	Sorrel or spinach	225 g
3 oz	Vegetable margarine	75 g
1½ lb	Trout fillets	700 g
	Salt and pepper	
5 tbsp	Plain wholemeal flour	5x15 ml
4 tbsp	Vegetable oil	4x15 ml
½ pint	Milk	300 ml
2 oz	Grated cheese	50 g
4 tbsp	Plain yogurt	4x15 ml

Preheat the oven to 425°F (220°C) Gas 7. Cut away blemishes and stalks from sorrel. Wash, then shred coarsely. Put 2 oz (50 g) of the margarine into a saucepan, add the sorrel, cover and cook gently for 5 minutes.

Meanwhile, wipe the fish fillets and remove the skin. Season 3 tbsp (3x15 ml) of the flour and use to coat the fish. Heat the oil in a frying pan, add the fish and fry for 2 minutes each side. Remove from the pan, drain and arrange in a shallow ovenproof dish.

Heat the remaining margarine in a saucepan, add remaining flour and cook for 1 minute. Gradually add the milk and bring to the boil, stirring constantly. Remove from the heat and beat in the cheese, sorrel and yogurt. Season to taste and spread over the fish.

Bake in the centre of the oven for 15 minutes till the fish is tender and the topping is golden brown. Serve immediately with new potatoes and a tomato salad.

Spanish-style cod fricassee

Overall timing 30 minutes

Freezing Suitable: reheat in double saucepan from frozen

To serve 6

6	Cod steaks	6
	Salt and pepper	
4 tbsp	Plain wholemeal flour	4x15 ml
4 tbsp	Vegetable oil	4x15 ml
1	Onion	1
1	Garlic clove	1
4 tbsp	Dry white wine	4x15 ml
4 tbsp	Water	4x15 ml
	Pinch of cayenne	
4 oz	Frozen peas	125 g
4 oz	Canned or frozen asparagus tips	125 g
1	Egg yolk	1
2 tbsp	Plain yogurt	2x15 ml
1 tbsp	Lemon juice	15 ml
2	Hard-boiled eggs	2

Wipe cod steaks and coat with seasoned flour. Heat oil in a frying pan. Add fish and cook for 8–10 minutes on each side. Remove fish from pan, place in serving dish and keep hot.

Peel and chop onion and garlic. Add to frying pan and cook till transparent. Stir in remaining seasoned flour, then pour in wine, water and pinch of cayenne. Simmer for 5 minutes, stirring frequently.

Add peas and asparagus tips to pan and cook over a low heat till tender. Mix egg yolk, yogurt and lemon juice in a bowl, then stir into pan. Cook for a few minutes but do not allow to boil. When mixture thickens remove pan from heat.

Pour sauce over fish, garnish with quartered hard-boiled eggs and serve with plain boiled rice or potatoes.

Caribbean fish with beans

Overall timing 2½ hours plus soaking

Freezing Not suitable

To serve 4

8 oz	Dried borlotti beans	225 g
1	Carrot	1
2	Garlic cloves	2
	Bouquet garni	
1	Onion	1
1	Red chilli	1
4 tbsp	Vegetable oil	4x15 ml
2 tbsp	Tomato purée	2x15 ml
2 tbsp	Water	2x15 ml
	Salt and pepper	
1½ lb	White fish fillets	700 g
3 tbsp	Plain wholemeal flour	3x15 ml

Wash beans, place in a large saucepan and cover with plenty of cold water. Bring to the boil for 2 minutes. Remove from heat, cover and leave to soak for 2 hours.

Scrape carrot. Peel 1 of the garlic cloves. Drain beans and return to pan with carrot, garlic and bouquet garni. Cover with boiling water and simmer for 2 hours until beans are tender.

Drain beans, discarding carrot, garlic and bouquet garni. Peel and chop onion. Deseed and finely chop chilli. Heat half the oil in a frying pan and fry the onion, chilli and remaining peeled and crushed garlic clove until golden. Stir in tomato purée and water. Add beans and seasoning. Cover and simmer gently for 10 minutes.

Meanwhile, wipe the fish fillets and cut into neat pieces. Toss in seasoned flour. Heat remaining oil in another frying pan and fry fish for 3–4 minutes on each side till golden.

Transfer bean mixture to a warmed serving dish. Taste and adjust seasoning. Arrange fried fish on top of beans and garnish with chopped parsley.

Fish with rice and vegetables

Overall timing 1¼ hours

Freezing Not suitable

To serve 4

4x8 oz	Firm-fleshed fish fillets	4x225 g
1	Garlic clove	1
2	Onions	2
3 tbsp	Chopped parsley	3x15 ml
3 tbsp	Lemon juice	3x15 ml
	Salt and pepper	
2	Medium-size carrots	2
1	Stalk of celery	1
1	Small cauliflower	1
8 oz	Cabbage	225 g
2 tbsp	Vegetable oil	2x15 ml
4 tbsp	Tomato purée	4x15 ml
1¾ pints	Water	1 litre
8 oz	Long grain brown rice	225 g

Wipe the fish fillets and remove skin. Peel and crush the garlic into a bowl. Peel and finely chop 1 of the onions. Add to the garlic with the parsley, lemon juice and seasoning. Mix well. Spread the mixture over the fish and leave to marinate for 30 minutes.

Meanwhile, scrape and thinly slice the carrots; peel and slice the remaining onion. Wash, trim and slice the celery; wash and trim the cauliflower and divide into florets. Wash and shred the cabbage.

Heat the oil in a flameproof casserole, add onion and fry till transparent. Stir in tomato purée and water and bring to the boil. Add the vegetables and rice. Bring back to the boil. Cover tightly and simmer for 15–20 minutes. Arrange the fish on top and simmer for 20 minutes longer till the fish and rice are tender and the liquid is absorbed.

Lift out the fish carefully. Place the rice and vegetables in a warmed serving dish and arrange the fish on top. Serve immediately.

Chinese-style prawns with peas

Overall timing 30 minutes

Freezing Not suitable

To serve 4

2 teasp	Cornflour	2x5 ml
1 tbsp	Soy sauce	15 ml
¼ pint	Strong chicken stock	150 ml
1 teasp	Muscovado sugar	5 ml
	Salt and pepper	
¼ teasp	Cayenne pepper	1.25 ml
2	Small onions	2
3 tbsp	Vegetable oil	3x15 ml
½ inch	Piece of root ginger	12.5 mm
1	Garlic clove	1
12 oz	Shelled prawns	350 g
8 oz	Frozen peas	225 g

To make the sauce, blend the cornflour, soy sauce, chicken stock, sugar, salt and cayenne in a bowl and reserve.

Peel the onions and cut through the root into 8 wedges. Heat the oil in a large frying pan, and stir-fry the onions over a high heat for 2 minutes. Finely shred or chop the ginger and add to the pan with the peeled and crushed garlic and the prawns. Stir-fry for 3 minutes.

Mix the sauce and pour into the pan. Bring to the boil, stirring constantly. Add the peas, cover and simmer for 3 minutes.

Adjust the seasoning to taste and pour into a warmed serving dish. Serve immediately with boiled brown rice.

Mussel bake

Overall timing 1 hour

Freezing Not suitable

To serve 4

4 oz	Lightly-toasted wholemeal bread	125 g
$\frac{1}{4}$ pint	Warm milk	150 ml
1	Onion	1
2 pints	Mussels	1.1 litres
5 tbsp	White wine	5x15 ml
1 oz	Melted vegetable margarine	25 g
4	Eggs	4
4 oz	Grated cheese	125 g
1 tbsp	Chopped parsley	15 ml
	Salt and pepper	
	Bran (optional)	

Preheat the oven to 375°F (190°C) Gas 5.

Break up the slices of bread and soak in the warm milk. Peel and chop the onion. Scrub and wash the mussels. Put into a saucepan with the wine, onion and margarine and cook over a high heat till the shells open. Discard any closed shells. Lift the mussels out of the pan with a draining spoon and remove from shells. Discard shells. Strain the cooking liquor through a muslin-lined sieve and reserve.

Beat the eggs in a bowl till frothy. Add the soaked breadcrumbs, cheese, mussels and reserved cooking liquor, the chopped parsley and seasoning. Mix well and pour into a greased 8 inch (20 cm) soufflé dish. Sprinkle with bran, if using.

Bake on the centre shelf of the oven for about 40 minutes till well risen and golden. Serve immediately.

Bobotie

Overall timing 1 hour 40 minutes

Freezing Not suitable

To serve 8

2 oz	Fresh wholemeal breadcrumbs	50 g
¼ pint	Milk	150 ml
2 oz	Dried apricots	50 g
3	Onions	3
2 oz	Vegetable margarine	50 g
2 teasp	Curry powder	2x5 ml
12	Split almonds	12
3 tbsp	Lemon juice	3x15 ml
	Salt	
2 teasp	Muscovado sugar	2x5 ml
2 oz	Seedless raisins	50 g
2 lb	Minced beef	900 g
2	Eggs	2
2	Bay leaves	2

Preheat the oven to 375°F (190°C) Gas 5.

Soak the breadcrumbs in half the milk. Chop the dried apricots. Peel and finely chop the onions. Melt the margarine in a frying pan and fry the onions for 3–4 minutes. Add curry powder and almonds and fry, stirring, for 1 minute. Add lemon juice, salt, sugar, dried apricots and raisins and simmer for 3 minutes.

Put the minced beef into a large bowl. Squeeze out the breadcrumbs and add to the beef with the mixture from the frying pan. Add one of the eggs and mix well.

Press the mixture into a greased ovenproof dish. Press the bay leaves into the mixture and smooth the top. Beat the remaining egg with the remaining milk, and pour over the meat. Bake for 45 minutes.

Serve hot with boiled rice and side dishes of coconut, and mango chutney.

Beef and dhal curry

Overall timing 2¼ hours

Freezing Not suitable

To serve 4

4oz	Egyptian lentils	125g
1 pint	Water	600ml
2	Dried chillies	2
1½lb	Chuck steak	700g
2	Medium onions	2
1	Garlic clove	1
2oz	Vegetable margarine	50g
2	Cardamom pods	2
2	Cloves	2
2 inch	Cinnamon stick	5cm
1 tbsp	Curry powder	15ml
1 tbsp	Tomato purée	15ml
	Salt	

Put lentils into a pan with ¾ pint (400ml) water and deseeded chillies. Bring to the boil and simmer for 10 minutes.

Meanwhile, cut meat into large cubes. Peel and finely chop onions; peel and crush garlic. Melt margarine in flameproof casserole, add onions and garlic and fry for 3 minutes. Lightly crush cardamom pods and add to pan with other spices and curry powder. Fry gently, stirring, for 3 minutes.

Drain the lentils, reserving the liquid. Discard the chillies.

Stir tomato purée and meat into casserole and fry till coated with spice mixture. Add cooking liquor from lentils. Bring to the boil, cover and simmer gently for about 1½ hours till beef is tender.

Add lentils and remaining water and simmer, uncovered, for a further 15 minutes till lentils become mushy and absorb the liquid. Discard cinnamon, cardamom and cloves. Add salt to taste, then serve with boiled rice.

Roast lamb and beans

Overall timing 1½ hours

Freezing Not suitable

To serve 4–6

3½ lb	Shoulder of lamb	1.6 kg
3	Garlic cloves	3
3 oz	Vegetable margarine	75 g
	Salt and pepper	
1	Bay leaf	1
4	Sprigs of thyme	4
14 oz	Can of flageolet or haricot beans	397 g
2 tbsp	Chopped parsley	2x15 ml

Preheat oven to 400°F (200°C) Gas 6.

Using a sharp knife, make slits in the lamb and insert slivers of 2 peeled garlic cloves. Smear lamb with 2 oz (50 g) of the margarine and season. Place bay leaf and thyme on top. Put meat into a roasting tin with 3 fl oz (90 ml) water and cook in oven, allowing 20 minutes per lb and 20 minutes over (40 minutes per kg plus 20 minutes). Turn off heat but leave meat to "rest" in oven for about 10 minutes before serving.

Meanwhile, drain beans (reserving liquid to make gravy with meat juices) and place in saucepan with remaining margarine, remaining garlic clove, crushed, and half the parsley. Heat through well, stirring occasionally, then place on warmed serving dish with lamb. Sprinkle with parsley and serve.

Lamb kebabs with prunes

Overall timing 50 minutes

Freezing Not suitable

To serve 4

12	Prunes	12
$\frac{1}{4}$ pint	Red wine	150 ml
1 lb	Lean lamb cut from the leg	450 g
3 tbsp	Oil	3x15 ml
	Salt and pepper	
$\frac{1}{2}$ teasp	Dried thyme	2.5 ml
2	Firm tomatoes	2
1	Medium onion	1
3	Thick rashers of streaky bacon	3

Put the prunes into a saucepan, add the red wine and bring to the boil. Remove from the heat and leave to soak for 30 minutes.

Cut lamb into 12 large cubes. Place in bowl with oil, seasoning and thyme. Cover and leave for 30 minutes.

Meanwhile, quarter the tomatoes. Peel the onion and cut through the root into eight wedges. Derind bacon and cut each rasher into four. Preheat the grill.

Drain the prunes, reserving the wine. Make a slit in each prune and remove the stone. Thread the lamb, prunes, tomatoes, bacon and onion on to four skewers. Brush the kebabs with the lamb marinade and the wine from the prunes, then sprinkle with salt and pepper. Grill for about 15 minutes, turning occasionally, till the lamb is tender. Arrange on a warmed serving dish and serve with boiled rice.

Spicy roast pork

Overall timing 3 hours

Freezing Not suitable

To serve 4

4 oz	Prunes	125 g
1	Large onion	1
1 oz	Vegetable margarine	25 g
2 tbsp	Vegetable oil	2 x 15 ml
1 tbsp	Five spice powder	15 ml
3 lb	Rolled pork spare rib roast	1.4 kg
	Salt and pepper	
½ pint	Stock	300 ml
4 oz	Sultanas	125 g
3 oz	Flaked almonds	75 g

Soak prunes in almost boiling water or strained tea.

Peel and chop onion. Heat margarine and oil in a flameproof casserole, add onion and five spices and cook till the onion is golden.

Season the pork. Add to casserole and brown on all sides over a high heat. Add stock, bring to the boil, cover and cook gently for 2 hours.

Drain prunes, remove stones and add to casserole with sultanas and almonds. Simmer for a further 30 minutes.

Place meat on a warmed serving dish and remove string. Surround with plain boiled rice and pour sauce over. Serve with yogurt mixed with chopped parsley, and mango chutney.

French vegetable stew

Overall timing 3 hours plus overnight soaking

Freezing Not suitable

To serve 6

8 oz	Dried haricot beans	225 g
4 pints	Water	2.2 litres
2	Carrots	2
1	Turnip	1
1	Onion	1
2	Leeks	2
2	Pig's knuckles	2
	Bouquet garni	
1	Garlic clove	1
	Salt and pepper	
8 oz	Potatoes	225 g
½	Small white cabbage	½
6	Slices of wholemeal bread	6
2 oz	Grated cheese	50 g

Soak beans overnight in water. The next day, drain and add 4 pints (2.2 litres) fresh water. Bring to the boil, cover and simmer for 1 hour.

Meanwhile, prepare vegetables. Peel and chop carrots, turnip and onion. Wash, trim and chop leeks. Add to pan with knuckles, bouquet garni, peeled garlic, salt and pepper. Cover and simmer for 1 hour.

Peel potatoes and cut into chunks. Wash and shred cabbage. Add to pan and cook for a further 30 minutes. Taste and adjust seasoning.

Preheat oven to 400°F (200°C) Gas 6. Remove both knuckles from pan and keep hot. Drain vegetables, saving cooking liquor, and place in ovenproof dish. Cover with bread slices and sprinkle with grated cheese. Spoon 4 tbsp (4x15ml) reserved stock over. Cook in oven for 10–15 minutes until cheese is golden. Serve meat separately.

Variation

After removing knuckles, cut meat off the bone. Return to pan, heat through, then serve.

Pork rings with kale

Overall timing 35 minutes

Freezing Not suitable

To serve 4

1½ lb	Floury potatoes	700 g
	Salt and pepper	
2 lb	Curly kale	900 g
2 x 8 oz	Smoked pork or frankfurter sausage rings	2 x 225 g
2 oz	Vegetable margarine	50 g
¼ pint	Milk	150 ml
¼ teasp	Grated nutmeg	1.25 ml

Peel the potatoes and cut into quarters. Put into a saucepan, cover with cold salted water and bring to the boil. Simmer for 10 minutes.

Meanwhile, wash the kale, remove any damaged leaves and tough stalks and shred finely. Bring a large pan of water to the boil, add the sausages and simmer for 10 minutes.

Add the kale to the potatoes and cook for a further 10 minutes till the potatoes are tender. Drain the vegetables thoroughly in a colander.

Put the margarine into the saucepan with the milk and heat till margarine melts. Return the vegetables to the pan and mash till smooth. Add the nutmeg and salt and pepper to taste. Spread on a warmed serving dish with a fork. Drain the sausages and arrange on the vegetables. Serve immediately.

Lentils with sausages

Overall timing 1¾ hours plus soaking

Freezing Not suitable

To serve 4–6

12 oz	Lentils	350 g
4 tbsp	Vegetable oil	4x15 ml
	Mixture of diced onion, celery, carrot and chopped parsley (to taste)	
8 oz	Can of tomatoes	225 g
	Salt and pepper	
	Hot stock	
1 lb	Sausages	450 g

Soak the lentils in cold water overnight. Drain.

Heat the oil in a flameproof casserole. Add the vegetable and parsley mixture and fry until beginning to brown. Add the lentils, tomatoes with their juice and seasoning. Cover and simmer gently, stirring occasionally, for 1½ hours or until the lentils are tender. Add hot stock from time to time to keep the mixture moist.

Just before the lentils are ready, cook the sausages under a preheated grill.

Pile the lentils in the centre of a warmed serving dish and surround with the sausages.

Neapolitan rice cake

Overall timing $2\frac{1}{4}$ hours

Freezing Not suitable

To serve 6

1 lb	Minced beef	450 g
2	Eggs	2
2 tbsp	Fresh wholemeal breadcrumbs	2x15 ml
5 tbsp	Grated Parmesan cheese	5x15 ml
	Salt and pepper	
1	Large onion	1
6 tbsp	Vegetable oil	6x15 ml
14 oz	Can of tomatoes	397 g
1¼ pints	Beef stock	700 ml
12 oz	Long grain brown rice	350 g
1 oz	Vegetable margarine	25 g
4 oz	Mozzarella cheese	125 g
4 oz	Cooked peas	125 g

Separate 1 of the eggs. Reserve white and mix yolk with beef, half the breadcrumbs, 1 tbsp (15 ml) Parmesan and salt and pepper. Shape into 1 inch (2.5 cm) balls.

Peel and finely chop onion. Heat 2 tbsp (2x15 ml) oil in a saucepan and fry onion till transparent. Add tomatoes and juice and bring to the boil. Simmer for 5 minutes.

Meanwhile, heat remaining oil in a frying pan, add meatballs and brown on all sides. Add drained meatballs to sauce and cook for 5 minutes. Remove with a draining spoon.

Add stock and bring to boil. Stir in rice and simmer for 40 minutes till rice is just tender. Remove from heat and beat in 2 tbsp (2x15 ml) Parmesan, egg white and whole egg. Cool.

Preheat oven to 400°F (200°C) Gas 6. Grease 8 inch (20 cm) loose-bottomed cake tin with half the margarine and sprinkle with remaining breadcrumbs. Spread three-quarters rice over the bottom and sides of tin. Dice Mozzarella. Arrange meatballs, peas, Mozzarella and remaining Parmesan in layers in tin. Cover with remaining rice and press down. Dot with remaining margarine and bake for 45 minutes.

Stuffed lettuce

Overall timing 45 minutes

Freezing Not suitable

To serve 4

2 oz	Fresh wholemeal breadcrumbs	50 g
¼ pint	Milk	150 ml
2	Onions	2
2	Garlic cloves	2
8 oz	Minced cooked meat	225 g
1 tbsp	Chopped parsley	15 ml
2	Hard-boiled eggs	2
1	Egg	1
	Salt and pepper	
4	Cos lettuces	4
2 tbsp	Vegetable oil	2x15 ml
14 oz	Can of tomatoes	397 g
2 tbsp	Tomato purée	2x15 ml
½ pint	Water	300 ml
	Bouquet garni	
¼ teasp	Ground cinnamon	1.25 ml

To make stuffing, soak breadcrumbs in milk. Peel and chop 1 onion and garlic clove. Mix with cooked meat and parsley. Shell and chop hard-boiled eggs. Add with squeezed out breadcrumbs, raw egg and seasoning. Mix well.

Trim lettuces, keeping them whole. Blanch in boiling salted water for 3 minutes, then drain thoroughly. Carefully open out lettuces and remove a few inside leaves. Spoon stuffing into cavity, then gently press lettuces back into shape.

Peel and finely chop remaining onion and garlic. Heat oil in a large saucepan and fry the onion and garlic until golden. Add tomatoes and their juice and mash well. Stir in tomato purée and water. Add bouquet garni, cinnamon and seasoning.

Add lettuces and bring to the boil. Cover and simmer for 20 minutes till tender. Cut each lettuce into thick slices and spoon sauce over to serve.

Traditional cassoulet

Overall timing 3½ hours plus 12 hours soaking

Freezing Suitable: add breadcrumbs and bake after thawing

To serve 6–8

1 lb	Dried haricot beans	450 g
1 lb	Belly of pork	450 g
4	Medium onions	4
6	Cloves	6
2	Carrots	2
2	Garlic cloves	2
2	Bouquet garni	2
2 pints	Stock	1.1 litre
1 lb	Boned lamb	450 g
1 oz	Vegetable margarine	25 g
14 oz	Can of tomatoes	397 g
2 tbsp	Tomato purée	2 x 15 ml
	Salt and pepper	
1 lb	Garlic sausage	450 g
4 oz	Wholemeal breadcrumbs	125 g

Soak beans overnight. Drain. Derind and dice belly pork. Peel two onions and spike each with cloves. Peel and chop carrots. Crush garlic. Put all into pan with one bouquet garni and stock. Cover and simmer for 1 hour.

Cube lamb. Peel and chop remaining onions. Melt margarine in a saucepan and brown lamb and onions. Stir in tomatoes, tomato purée, remaining bouquet garni and seasoning. Cover and simmer for 30 minutes.

Preheat the oven to 325°F (170°C) Gas 3.

Remove spiked onions and bouquet garni from beans. Using a draining spoon, place a layer of beans in greased ovenproof casserole. Cover with half lamb mixture. Dice sausage and put half on top. Continue layers, finishing with beans. Pour over stock from beans; reserve rest. Sprinkle crumbs on top and bake for 1 hour 40 minutes. Add a little more stock if the cassoulet becomes too dry.

Liver with sultanas

Overall timing 20 minutes

Freezing Not suitable

To serve 4

1 lb	Calves' or lamb's liver	450 g
2 tbsp	Vegetable oil	2 x 15 ml
1 oz	Vegetable margarine	25 g
2 oz	Sultanas	50 g
1 tbsp	Plain wholemeal flour	15 ml
1 tbsp	Red wine vinegar	15 ml
$\frac{1}{4}$ pint	Water	150 ml
	Salt and pepper	

Cut the liver into 8 slices. Heat the oil and margarine in a frying pan, add liver and fry for 3–4 minutes each side till tender. Remove from pan with draining spoon and arrange on warmed serving dish. Keep hot.

Toss the sultanas in the flour and add to the frying pan. Fry, stirring, for 3 minutes. Add vinegar, water and seasoning to taste. Cook for a further 3 minutes, stirring continuously. Pour the juices over the liver and serve with boiled potatoes.

Sweetbreads with peas

Overall timing 1 hour 35 minutes

Freezing Not suitable

To serve 4

2 lb	Fresh peas	900 g
1	Large round lettuce	1
4 oz	Button onions	125 g
4 oz	Vegetable margarine	125 g
1 teasp	Muscovado sugar	5 ml
	Salt and pepper	
1	Large carrot	1
1	Large onion	1
2 oz	Plain wholemeal flour	50 g
$\frac{3}{4}$ pint	Chicken stock	400 ml
1 teasp	Tomato purée	5 ml
2	Prepared calves' sweetbreads	2

Shell and wash peas. Trim and wash lettuce and quarter. Peel button onions. Put into a large saucepan with 2 oz (50 g) of the mar-garine, 1 tbsp (15 ml) water, the sugar and seasoning. Cover and bring to boil. Simmer for 40 minutes.

Meanwhile, scrape and slice the carrot; peel and finely chop the large onion. Heat 1 oz (25 g) of the margarine in a large saucepan, add the carrot and onion and fry till lightly browned. Add half the flour and cook for 1 minute, then gradually stir in the stock. Bring to the boil, stirring constantly. Add the tomato purée and seasoning and simmer uncovered for 15 minutes.

Heat the remaining margarine in a frying pan. Coat the sweetbreads with the remaining flour, add to the pan and fry till golden brown all over. Drain and add to the stock. Bring to the boil, cover and simmer for 30 minutes till tender.

Arrange the peas, lettuce and button onions on a warmed serving dish. Drain the sweet-breads and arrange on top. Strain the cooking liquor, adjust the seasoning to taste and spoon over the sweetbreads. Serve immediately with creamed potatoes.

Braised tripe with beans

Overall timing 3 hours plus soaking

Freezing Not suitable

To serve 4–6

8 oz	Dried haricot beans	225 g
2 lb	Honeycomb tripe	900 g
	Milk	
	Salt and pepper	
1 oz	Salt pork	25 g
1	Small onion	1
1	Stalk of celery	1
1	Small carrot	1
2 oz	Vegetable margarine	50 g
14 oz	Can of tomatoes	400 g
1	Bouquet garni	1

Soak the beans in cold water overnight. Drain. Put into a saucepan, cover with fresh cold water and bring to the boil. Simmer for about 1 hour or until tender.

Meanwhile, place the tripe in a saucepan and cover with a mixture of milk and water. Add a pinch of salt, then cover and simmer for 1 hour.

Soak the salt pork in cold water for 1 hour, then drain and cut into cubes.

Peel and chop the onion. Trim and dice the celery. Scrape and slice the carrot. Melt the margarine in a flameproof casserole and fry the vegetables with the salt pork until softened.

Drain the tripe, reserving 5 tbsp (5x15 ml) of the cooking liquid. Cut into strips and add to the vegetables with the reserved liquid, tomatoes sieved with their juice, bouquet garni and seasoning. Cook gently for about 1½ hours.

Fifteen minutes before the tripe has finished cooking, add the drained beans. Adjust the seasoning and discard the bouquet garni before serving.

Chicken stuffed with nuts and currants

Overall timing

Freezing Not suitable

To serve 4

1 oz	Sultanas	25 g
3 lb	Ovenready chicken	1.4 kg
	Salt and pepper	
5 tbsp	Vegetable oil	5x15 ml
2 oz	Vegetable margarine	50 g
2 oz	Dried wholemeal breadcrumbs	50 g
$\frac{1}{2}$ pint	Chicken stock	300 ml
2 tbsp	Wine vinegar	2x15 ml
2 oz	Redcurrants	50 g
1 oz	Chopped walnuts	25 g
1 oz	Chopped hazelnuts	25 g
1 oz	Pine nuts	25 g
1 oz	Ground almonds	25 g
2 teasp	Muscovado sugar	2x5 ml

Place sultanas in a bowl, cover with warm water and leave to swell.

Wash chicken and dry well. Season inside and out with salt and pepper. Heat the oil and 1 oz (25 g) of the margarine in a flameproof casserole and brown the chicken on all sides over a high heat. Remove from heat. Preheat oven to 375°F (190°C) Gas 5.

Melt remaining margarine in a saucepan and stir in breadcrumbs. Brown them evenly, stirring with a wooden spoon, over a low heat. Drain sultanas and add to pan. Pour in 2 fl oz (60 ml) stock and add the wine vinegar, half the redcurrants, the nuts, sugar and $\frac{1}{4}$ teasp (1.25 ml) salt. Bring to the boil and simmer for 2–3 minutes. Moisten with more stock if mixture becomes too dry.

Stuff chicken with the mixture and close with needle and thread or with skewers. Place chicken in casserole and pour over remaining stock. Cover and cook in oven for 1 hour, basting from time to time. Add more stock if too much evaporation occurs.

Place chicken on serving plate. Garnish with remaining redcurrants.

Braised stuffed chicken

Overall timing 2½ hours

Freezing Suitable: broth only

To serve 6

4 oz	Stale wholemeal breadcrumbs	125 g
¼ pint	Milk	150 ml
5 oz	Cooked ham	150 g
	Parsley	
8 oz	Sausagemeat	225 g
¼ teasp	Dried thyme	1.25 ml
	Grated nutmeg	
1	Egg	1
	Salt and pepper	
3 lb	Ovenready chicken	1.4 kg
2 tbsp	Lemon juice	2x15 ml
	Chicken stock	
4	Carrots	4
1 lb	Potatoes	450 g
1	Small stalk of celery	1
6	Small leeks	6

To make stuffing: soak breadcrumbs in milk for 5 minutes, then squeeze out excess liquid. Chop ham and a few sprigs of parsley very finely. Mix with squeezed-out breadcrumbs, sausagemeat, thyme, pinch of grated nutmeg and egg. Season generously.

Rinse and dry chicken. Stuff with prepared mixture. Sew up opening with needle and string, then truss if wished. Brush all over with lemon juice.

Bring enough stock to cover chicken completely to the boil in large pan and put in chicken, breast side up. Simmer for 1½ hours.

Meanwhile, peel carrots and potatoes and leave whole. Trim celery and leeks and halve or quarter. Add vegetables to chicken and cook 30 minutes longer.

Lift out chicken and place on warmed serving dish. Untruss. Arrange vegetables around chicken. Serve some of the broth as a gravy separately, the rest as a soup.

Moroccan chicken

Overall timing 1¼ hours

Freezing Not suitable

To serve 6

6	Chicken portions	6
2	Large onions	2
6 tbsp	Vegetable oil	6x15ml
¼ teasp	Powdered saffron	1.25ml
	Salt and pepper	
1½ pints	Water	850ml
2	Sprigs of fresh coriander	2
1lb	Precooked couscous	450g
6	Hard-boiled eggs	6
2oz	Flaked almonds	50g

Wash and trim the chicken portions. Peel and chop the onions. Melt 4 tbsp (4x15ml) oil in a flameproof casserole, add onions and fry for 3 minutes. Add the chicken portions and fry over a moderate heat till lightly browned all over. Add the saffron, seasoning and water.

Wash the coriander and tie the sprigs together. Add to the pan and bring to the boil. Half cover the pan and simmer for about 45 minutes, stirring occasionally, till tender.

Meanwhile, cook the couscous according to the instructions on the packet or steam over boiling water for 30 minutes.

Lift the chicken out of the sauce and keep hot. Boil the sauce till reduced by one third and season to taste. Shell eggs and cut in half lengthways. Heat the remaining oil in a frying pan and fry the almonds till crisp and golden.

Pile the couscous on a warmed serving dish and arrange the chicken on top. Spoon the sauce over and garnish with the hard-boiled eggs. Sprinkle with the fried almonds and serve.

Chicken with lentils

Overall timing 1¼ hours

Freezing Not suitable

To serve 6

12 oz	Continental lentils	350 g
1	Onion	1
1	Carrot	1
	Bouquet garni	
	Salt and pepper	
1 lb	Boned chicken	450 g
1 tbsp	Vegetable oil	15 ml
3 oz	Vegetable margarine	75 g
1 tbsp	Chopped parsley	15 ml

Wash and pick over lentils. Place in a saucepan and add enough cold water just to cover. Peel and finely chop onion. Peel and halve carrot. Add to lentils with bouquet garni and seasoning. Bring to boil, cover and simmer for 35 minutes.

Meanwhile, cut chicken into neat pieces. Heat oil and half the margarine in a frying pan, add chicken pieces and fry for 5 minutes, turning once. Add chicken to lentils, cover and simmer for a further 30 minutes.

Discard bouquet garni and carrot. Stir the remaining margarine into lentils. Taste and adjust seasoning. Arrange chicken and lentils on a warmed serving dish and sprinkle with parsley. Serve immediately with a mixed salad.

Sweet and sour chicken

Overall timing 1¼ hours

Freezing Not suitable

To serve 4-6

8	Chicken joints	8
	Salt and pepper	
3 tbsp	Vegetable oil	3x15 ml
9 fl oz	Hot chicken stock	250 ml
8 oz	Can of pineapple pieces	227 g
2 oz	Vegetable margarine	50 g
4 oz	Flaked almonds	125 g
2	Bananas	2
1	Orange	1
4 oz	Cocktail cherries	110 g
2 tbsp	Mild curry powder	2x15 ml
2 tbsp	Cornflour	2x15 ml
4 fl oz	Plain yogurt	113 ml

Preheat oven to 375°F (190°C) Gas 5. Wash and dry chicken joints. Rub with salt and pepper. Heat the oil in flameproof casserole and brown joints on all sides. Put the chicken in the oven and cook, uncovered, for 40 minutes. Baste with stock frequently.

Meanwhile, drain the pineapple and save the juice. Melt margarine in a saucepan, add almonds and cook till golden brown. Peel and slice bananas and orange and add to almonds with drained cherries and pineapple pieces. Turn mixture over, heat through then remove from heat.

Remove casserole from the oven. Place the chicken pieces on a warm serving dish. Cover with the fruit and almond mixture and keep warm. Combine any remaining chicken stock with chicken juices and pineapple juice. Make up to ¾ pint (400 ml) with water.

In saucepan, mix curry powder and cornflour to a smooth paste. Gradually stir in measured liquid. Bring to the boil, stirring, and cook for 1–2 minutes. Remove from heat and stir in yogurt. Pour some of the sauce over the chicken; put the remainder in a sauceboat.

Roast stuffed turkey

Overall timing 4½ hours

Freezing Not suitable

To serve 15

12–14lb	Turkey	about 6kg
8oz	Streaky bacon	225g
1½ pints	Turkey giblet stock	900ml
2 tbsp	Plain wholemeal flour	2x15ml
Stuffing		
1	Onion	1
1lb	Sausagemeat	450g
4oz	Chopped mixed nuts	125g
2oz	Sultanas	50g
2 teasp	Dried mixed herbs	2x5ml
4oz	Fresh wholemeal breadcrumbs	125g
2	Eggs	2
	Salt and pepper	

Preheat oven to 450°F (230°C) Gas 8. Peel and chop onion and mix with remaining stuffing ingredients. Use half to stuff turkey. Roll rest into balls and place in a small greased dish. Rub salt and pepper into turkey.

Place rack in roasting tin and arrange half bacon slices on top. Put turkey, breast down, on bacon. Arrange remaining bacon slices on top of turkey. Roast for 20 minutes.

Baste turkey well with pan juices. Add ½ pint (300ml) stock to pan. Cover turkey legs with foil. Reduce heat to 350°F (180°C) Gas 4 and roast for a further hour. Baste every 15 minutes.

Turn turkey breast side up. Roast, basting regularly, for about 2 hours. An hour before end of cooking time, place dish of stuffing balls in oven.

Put turkey on to a heatproof serving dish and leave in a warm place for 20 minutes before carving. Make gravy from pan juices, flour and remaining stock.

Spinach and carrot mould

Overall timing 2 hours

Freezing Not suitable

To serve 6–8

1 lb	Spinach	450 g
3	Eggs	3
2 oz	Vegetable margarine	50 g
2 tbsp	Plain wholemeal flour	2x15 ml
6 fl oz	Milk	175 ml
	Salt and pepper	
	Grated nutmeg	
2 tbsp	Grated Parmesan cheese	2x15 ml
8 oz	Carrots	225 g

Preheat the oven to 350°F (180°C) Gas 4. Rinse the spinach well, then cook in the water clinging to the leaves until tender. Drain well and sieve or purée in a blender. Separate the eggs, and beat 1 yolk into the spinach purée.

Melt the margarine in a saucepan. Stir in the flour and cook for 1 minute, then gradually stir in the milk. Bring to the boil, stirring, and simmer until thickened. Add seasoning and nutmeg to taste.

Add half the sauce to the spinach mixture, with 1 tbsp (15 ml) of the cheese. Mix well and leave to cool.

Meanwhile, scrape the carrots and cook in boiling salted water until very tender. Drain and sieve or purée in a blender. Add the remaining sauce, egg yolks and cheese and mix well. Cool.

Beat 1 egg white until stiff and fold into the spinach mixture. Beat the remaining egg whites until stiff and fold into the carrot mixture. Pour the spinach mixture into a greased large soufflé dish and smooth the top, then cover with the carrot mixture. Place in a roasting tin of hot water and bake for 1 hour. Unmould and serve immediately.

Vegetable and bacon risotto

Overall timing 2¾ hours plus soaking

Freezing Not suitable

To serve 4–6

6 oz	Dried red kidney beans	175 g
12 oz	Cabbage	350 g
2	Stalks of celery	2
1	Carrot	1
3	Tomatoes	3
4 pints	Water	2.2 litres
1	Small onion	1
4 oz	Bacon	100 g
1 oz	Vegetable margarine	25 g
12 oz	Brown rice	350 g
	Salt and pepper	
	Bran (optional)	

Soak the beans in cold water overnight. Drain. Rinse, core and shred the cabbage. Trim and chop the celery. Scrape and chop the carrot. Chop the tomatoes. Put all the vegetables in a large saucepan with the water and bring to the boil. Cover and simmer gently for 2 hours.

Peel and chop the onion. Derind and dice the bacon. Heat the margarine in a frying pan and fry the onion and bacon until golden. Add the rice and cook, stirring, until translucent.

Add the rice mixture to the saucepan and stir well. Simmer, uncovered, until the rice is tender and all the liquid has been absorbed. Season well, sprinkle with bran, if using, and serve.

Stuffed courgettes

Overall timing 1½ hours

Freezing Suitable: bake from frozen, covered, in 350°F (180°C) Gas 4 oven for about 45 minutes or till hot

To serve 4

5 oz	Mixed cooked chicken and ham *or*	150 g
3½ oz	Can of tuna	100 g
2 tbsp	Chopped parsley	2x15 ml
1	Garlic clove	1
4 tbsp	Fresh wholemeal breadcrumbs	4x15 ml
2 tbsp	Grated cheese	2x15 ml
1	Egg	1
4	Large courgettes	4
14 oz	Can of tomatoes	397 g
1 tbsp	Vegetable oil	15 ml
2 teasp	Dried basil	2x5 ml

Finely chop chicken and ham, or drain tuna, discarding oil, and mash with a fork. In a bowl, mix together the meat, or tuna, parsley, peeled and crushed garlic, 2 tbsp (2x15 ml) breadcrumbs, cheese and egg.

Wash courgettes and trim ends. Halve them lengthways. Scoop out centres with a melon baller or small spoon, chop finely and add to bowl. Fill courgette shells with prepared mixture.

Purée drained tomatoes in a blender or push through a sieve. Heat oil in a flameproof casserole, add tomato purée and basil and cook for about 10 minutes. Meanwhile heat the oven to 350°F (180°C) Gas 4.

Add stuffed courgettes to casserole, sprinkle with remaining breadcrumbs, baste with tomato sauce, cover and cook in the oven for 50 minutes. Remove lid for last 10 minutes of cooking to help crisp the topping. Serve hot.

Spinach roll

Overall timing 2 hours

Freezing Not suitable

To serve 4-6

12 oz	Plain flour	350 g
	Salt	
2	Eggs	2
Filling		
1 lb	Spinach	450 g
6 oz	Cottage cheese	175 g
6 oz	Grated Parmesan cheese	175 g
2	Eggs	2
	Grated nutmeg	

Sift the flour and 1 teasp (5 ml) salt into a bowl. Make a well in the centre and add the eggs. Mix together, adding enough lukewarm water to make a soft dough. Chill for 30 minutes.

Meanwhile, rinse the spinach and cook in the water that clings to the leaves until tender. Drain well, then sieve or purée in a blender with the cottage cheese. Beat in the Parmesan cheese, eggs, and salt and nutmeg to taste.

Roll out the dough to a thin rectangle and spread over the spinach mixture, leaving a border clear all round. Roll up like a Swiss roll. Roll up in a clean cloth and tie the ends with string.

Cook in simmering salted water for about 1 hour. Unwrap and place on a warm serving dish. Slice and serve with hot tomato sauce.

Marrow with tomato sauce

Overall timing 1 hour

Freezing Not suitable

To serve 4

2 oz	Fresh wholemeal breadcrumbs	50 g
3½ lb	Vegetable marrow	1.6 kg
1 tbsp	Vegetable margarine	15 ml
3 tbsp	Vegetable oil	3x15 ml
1	Onion	1
2	Garlic cloves	2
4 tbsp	Plain wholemeal flour	4x15 ml
1 teasp	Salt	5 ml
4 tbsp	Tomato purée	4x15 ml
1 pint	Stock	560 ml
	Cayenne pepper	
2 oz	Grated Parmesan cheese	50 g

Preheat oven to 375°F (190°C) Gas 5. Grease bottom of ovenproof dish. Sprinkle crumbs over bottom. Blanch marrow for a few minutes in boiling water, then peel and cut into quarters. Remove seeds and cut flesh into 1 inch (2.5 cm) cubes.

Heat margarine and 1 tbsp (15 ml) of the oil in saucepan. Peel and chop onion. Add half to the pan with the marrow, and cook, stirring occasionally, for 20 minutes. Remove marrow with a draining spoon and place in greased ovenproof dish.

Add rest of oil to pan and cook rest of onion with peeled and crushed garlic. When soft, add flour and salt and cook for 1–2 minutes without browning. Remove from heat and gradually add the tomato purée and stock, stirring continuously. Return to heat and bring to the boil, stirring all the time till the sauce thickens. Add a pinch of cayenne pepper.

Pour sauce over marrow, then sprinkle with the grated Parmesan. Bake for 30–40 minutes till golden brown. Serve with crisp green salad and wholemeal rolls.

Aubergine bake

Overall timing 1 hour

Freezing Not suitable

To serve 4–6

1¼ lb	Aubergines	600 g
1 lb	Onions	450 g
4 fl oz	Vegetable oil	120 ml
2 teasp	Salt	2x5 ml
1 teasp	Cayenne pepper	5 ml
1 tbsp	Tomato purée	15 ml
15 oz	Can of chick peas	425 g
2 lb	Very ripe tomatoes	900 g

Preheat the oven to 400°F (200°C) Gas 6. Wash the aubergines. Remove the stalks and cut into ¾ inch (2 cm) thick slices. Peel and thickly slice onions. Heat half the oil in a frying pan until very hot. Add the aubergine, in batches, and brown on both sides. Add more oil as necessary. Remove the aubergines and arrange in a large but shallow ovenproof dish or roating tin.

Add a little more oil to the frying pan and cook the onion slices till soft and golden brown, then spread on top of the aubergines.

Combine salt, cayenne pepper, tomato purée and ¾ pint (400 ml) water together. Pour over mixture. Drain chick peas and scatter over the top. Cover with foil, then bake on middle shelf of oven for 20 minutes.

Meanwhile, skin and quarter tomatoes. Remove dish from oven and place tomatoes round edges of dish. Cover again and cook for further 25 minutes, or until tender.

When cooked, remove from oven and allow to go cold. Serve with pitta or French bread and a cucumber and yogurt salad if you wish to add a crunchy touch to your meal.

Vegetable moussaka

Overall timing 2 hours

Freezing Not suitable

To serve 4–6

2	Large onions	2
1	Garlic clove	1
1	Large aubergine	1
	Salt and pepper	
2 oz	Vegetable margarine	50 g
4 oz	Continental lentils	125 g
2 tbsp	Tomato purée	2x15 ml
1 pint	Light stock	560 ml
4	Small globe artichokes	4
1 tbsp	Lemon juice	15 ml
	Bouquet garni	
4 tbsp	Vegetable oil	4x15 ml
	Sprigs of parsley	

Peel and finely chop onions; peel and crush garlic. Slice aubergine, sprinkle with salt and leave to drain for 15 minutes.

Melt the margarine in a saucepan, add onion and garlic and fry till golden. Add lentils, tomato purée and stock and simmer for about 1 hour till a thick purée.

Meanwhile, remove stem and coarse outer leaves from artichokes. Bring a pan of water to the boil, add lemon juice, bouquet garni and artichokes and simmer for 20–30 minutes till tender.

Rinse aubergines and dry on kitchen paper. Heat oil in a frying pan, add aubergines and fry till crisp and golden.

Preheat oven to 350°F (180°C) Gas 4.

Drain artichokes thoroughly, cut in half and remove chokes. Arrange cut sides up in greased ovenproof dish. Pour half lentil mixture over artichokes, then cover with half fried aubergine slices. Repeat the layers of lentil and aubergine and press down lightly. Bake for 30 minutes. Turn out and serve hot, garnished with parsley.

Spring vegetable pie

Overall timing 2 hours

Freezing Not suitable

To serve 6

1 lb	Spring greens	450 g
2	Small globe artichokes	2
1½ lb	Fresh peas	700 g
	Salt and pepper	
1	Large onion	1
3 oz	Vegetable margarine	75 g
8 oz	Wholemeal shortcrust pastry	225 g
4	Eggs	4
4 tbsp	Grated Parmesan cheese	4x15 ml
1 tbsp	Chopped parsley	15 ml

Pick over the spring greens, discarding any damaged parts, and chop coarsely. Remove stems and tough outer leaves from artichokes and cut artichokes into quarters, discarding the hairy chokes. Shell peas. Bring a pan of lightly salted water to the boil, add the artichokes and peas and simmer for 10 minutes.

Peel and chop onion. Melt margarine in large saucepan, add onion and fry till golden.

Drain artichokes and peas and add to the onion with the spring greens and seasoning. Mix well, cover tightly and simmer for 10 minutes, shaking the pan occasionally. Cool.

Preheat oven to 400°F (200°C) Gas 6.

Roll out two-thirds of dough and use to line an 8 inch (20 cm) springform tin. Spread vegetables in tin. Beat three of the eggs lightly with cheese and parsley, then pour over vegetables. Roll out remaining dough and cover filling. Beat remaining egg and brush over pie. Place tin on a baking tray and bake for 30 minutes.

Remove sides of tin. Brush sides of pie with egg and bake for a further 10–15 minutes till golden.

Dutch baked cabbage

Overall timing 45 minutes

Freezing Not suitable

To serve 4

1	White cabbage	1
8 fl oz	Hot stock	220 ml
8 fl oz	Water	220 ml
1	Bay leaf	1
1	Garlic clove	1
1	Onion	1
2	Cloves	2
	Salt and pepper	
2 oz	Vegetable margarine	50 g
3 tbsp	Plain wholemeal flour	3x15 ml
1 teasp	Curry powder	5 ml
8 fl oz	Plain yogurt	220 ml
2 tbsp	Wholemeal breadcrumbs	2x15 ml

Preheat the oven to 425°F (220°C) Gas 7.

Cut out core and remove tough outer leaves of cabbage. Stand cabbage upright in a saucepan. Pour over stock and water and add bay leaf, garlic and onion spiked with cloves. Seaon with salt and pepper.

Bring to the boil, then cover and simmer for about 10 minutes. Carefully lift out the cabbage and cut it into wedges. Place these in a greased ovenproof dish. Reserve ½ pint (300 ml) of the strained cooking liquor.

Melt the margarine in a saucepan. Stir in the flour and curry powder and cook for 1 minute. Gradually stir in the reserved cooking liquor and bring to the boil. Simmer, stirring, till thickened. Season sauce with salt and stir in yogurt.

Pour sauce over cabbage and sprinkle top with breadcrumbs. Bake for 15 minutes till top is lightly browned.

Spanish omelette torte

Overall timing 50 minutes

Freezing Not suitable

To serve 4

6	Eggs	6
1 oz	Plain wholemeal flour	25 g
3 tbsp	Milk	3x15 ml
2 tbsp	Grated Parmesan cheese	2x15 ml
	Salt and pepper	
2	Carrots	2
4 oz	Frozen peas	100 g
1	Onion	1
2 oz	Vegetable margarine	50 g

Lightly beat the eggs with the flour, milk, cheese and seasoning. Set aside.

Scrape and dice the carrots. Cook in a little boiling salted water with the peas until almost tender. Drain well.

Peel and chop the onion. Melt half the margarine in a small frying pan and fry the onion until golden. Add the carrots and peas and mix well, then add to the egg mixture.

Melt the remaining margarine in a round, flameproof baking tin. Pour in the egg mixture and cook gently for 20 minutes or until the torte is set on the bottom. Meanwhile, preheat the oven to 400°F (200°C) Gas 6.

Place the tin in the oven and bake until the torte is set and golden on top. Cool in the tin, then turn out and serve cold.

Swiss style potatoes

Overall timing 1 hour

Freezing Not suitable

To serve 4

2 lb	Potatoes	900 g
3 tbsp	Caraway seeds	3 x 15 ml
1 tbsp	Sea-salt	15 ml
2 oz	Vegetable margarine	50 g
8 oz	Curd cheese	225 g
4 fl oz	Milk	120 ml
1	Onion	1
2 tbsp	Chopped parsley	2 x 15 ml
2 tbsp	Chopped mustard and cress	2 x 15 ml
	Salt and pepper	
Garnish		
	Parsley sprigs	
	Mustard and cress	

Preheat the oven to 350°F (180°C) Gas 4.

Halve potatoes. Mix caraway seeds and sea-salt together in a bowl. Dip the cut sides of potatoes into mixture. Place potatoes in greased ovenproof dish with the caraway seeds facing up.

Melt the margarine and pour a little over each potato half. Bake for 45 minutes.

Mix cheese with milk in a bowl. Peel and finely chop onion and add to bowl with parsley, mustard and cress and seasoning.

Divide cheese mixture between warmed serving plates and place the potatoes on top. Garnish with parsley and cress.

Baked eggs in potatoes

Overall timing 2 hours

Freezing Not suitable

To serve 4

4x10oz	Potatoes	4x275g
2oz	Vegetable margarine	50g
	Salt and pepper	
2oz	Cheese	50g
4	Small eggs	4
4 tbsp	Plain yogurt	4x15ml
2 teasp	Chopped chives	2x5ml

Preheat the oven to 400°F (200°C) Gas 6.

Scrub and dry the potatoes and push a metal skewer lengthways through each one. Place on a baking tray and rub a little of the margarine over the skins. Bake for 1–1¼ hours.

Remove from the oven. Increase the temperature to 450°F (230°C) Gas 8.

Cut a slice lengthways off each potato and scoop out the insides, leaving a shell about ½ inch (12.5mm) thick. Mash the scooped-out potato (plus any from the lids) in a bowl with the remaining margarine and seasoning. Grate cheese and beat into potato mixture.

Press the mixture back into the potato shells, leaving a hollow in the centre large enough for an egg. Place on baking tray. Carefully break an egg into each potato. Season and spoon the yogurt over. Return to the oven and bake for 8–10 minutes till the eggs are lightly set. Sprinkle the chives over and serve hot.

French-style peas

Overall timing 50 minutes

Freezing Not suitable

To serve 4

2 lb	Fresh peas	900 g
8	Button onions	8
1	Large round lettuce	1
2 oz	Vegetable margarine	50 g
1	Sprig of fresh parsley	1
1	Sprig of fresh mint	1
2 teasp	Muscovado sugar	2x5 ml
	Salt and pepper	
$\frac{1}{4}$ pint	Hot stock	150 ml

Preheat the oven to 350°F (180°C) Gas 4. Shell the peas. Peel the onions. Wash the lettuce and cut into quarters.

Place margarine and herbs in casserole and add the peas and onions. Arrange lettuce on top. Sprinkle with sugar, salt and pepper, then pour over the hot stock.

Cover and bake in centre of oven for 35–40 minutes.

Mexican-style corn

Overall timing 20 minutes

Freezing Not suitable

To serve 4–6

1 lb	Frozen sweetcorn kernels	450 g
4	Tomatoes	4
1	Green pepper	1
1	Red pepper	1
1	Chilli	1
3 tbsp	Vegetable oil	3 x 15 ml
	Salt	
	Cayenne pepper	

Thaw and drain sweetcorn. Blanch, peel and finely chop tomatoes. Wash, deseed and finely chop peppers and chilli.

Heat oil in a frying pan. Cook tomatoes, peppers and chilli for 10 minutes. Season with salt and cayenne, then add sweetcorn. Heat through, shaking the pan to prevent sticking. Serve hot.

Broad beans with savory

Overall timing 35 minutes

Freezing Not suitable

To serve 4

2 lb	Fresh broad beans	900 g
1	Sprig of fresh savory	1
	Salt and pepper	
2 oz	Vegetable margarine	50 g
1 tbsp	Lemon juice	15 ml
1 tbsp	Chopped fresh or dried savory	15 ml

Shell beans, reserving 1 pod. Put beans, pod and sprig of savory into pan of boiling salted water, cover and simmer for 10–15 minutes till tender.

Drain beans, discarding pod and savory. Melt margarine gently in pan, add lemon juice, pepper and beans and toss till coated. Arrange in serving dish and sprinkle with chopped savory.

Tuscany beans

Overall timing 2 hours plus overnight soaking

Freezing Suitable

To serve 4

12 oz	Dried haricot beans	350 g
	Salt and pepper	
3 tbsp	Vegetable oil	3 x 15 ml
2	Garlic cloves	2
6	Leaves of fresh sage	6
7½ oz	Can of Italian plum tomatoes	213 g
1 tbsp	Tomato purée	15 ml

Soak beans overnight, then bring to the boil in the soaking water and cook for 5 minutes. Tip into a colander or sieve and wash beans under cold running water.

Return beans to pan, cover with fresh cold water, bring to the boil and simmer for 50 minutes. Add 1 teasp (5 ml) salt halfway through cooking time. Drain well.

Heat the oil in a flameproof casserole, add peeled and crushed garlic, drained beans and 2 of the sage leaves. Cook for 5 minutes.

Mash tomatoes and juice and stir into the casserole with tomato purée and seasoning. Cover and simmer for 30 minutes. Decorate with remaining sage leaves and serve immediately.

Italian chickpea salad

Overall timing 15 minutes plus chilling time

Freezing Not suitable

To serve 4

2	Small onions	2
8 oz	Mozzarella cheese	225 g
12 oz	Cooked chickpeas	350 g
1 teasp	Prepared mustard	5 ml
2 tbsp	Vinegar	2 x 15 ml
	Salt and pepper	
1 tbsp	Lemon juice	15 ml
4 tbsp	Vegetable oil	4 x 15 ml
2	Hard-boiled eggs	2

Peel onions and cut into rings. Dice the Mozzarella. Put into a salad bowl with the cooked chickpeas, mustard, vinegar and seasoning. Sprinkle with the lemon juice and oil and mix well together.

Chill salad for 30 minutes, then serve garnished with hard-boiled eggs, cut into quarters or eighths.

Mediterranean salad

Overall timing 15 minutes

Freezing Not suitable

To serve 4–6

2	Green peppers	2
1	Small onion	1
1	Garlic clove	1
1 tbsp	Dijon mustard	15 ml
1 tbsp	Dried mixed herbs	15 ml
6 tbsp	Vegetable oil	6x15 ml
2 tbsp	Lemon juice	2x15 ml
2 tbsp	Vinegar	2x15 ml
	Salt and pepper	
1 lb	Cooked chickpeas	450 g
2 oz	Can of anchovy fillets	57 g
2 oz	Black olives	50 g
	Chopped parsley	

Deseed peppers and cut into thin strips. Peel and finely chop onion.

Rub the peeled and cut garlic clove around the inside of a salad bowl. Add the onion, mustard, herbs, 2 tbsp (2x15 ml) of the oil, the lemon juice and seasoning. Mix together well. Pour the dressing into a basin and set aside.

Put the rest of the oil and the vinegar into the salad bowl. Season with salt and pepper and beat with a fork. Add the pepper slices and cooked chickpeas. Toss till coated in the dressing. Garnish with drained anchovy fillets, olives and parsley. Pour over the herb dressing and serve.

Variation

Mix an equal amount of cooked red kidney beans and white haricot beans with the chickpeas, or, instead of kidney beans, use freshly cooked green beans cut into 1 inch (2.5 cm) lengths. Add a little cooked sweetcorn to the salad or some chopped celery. Another chickpea salad can be made by mixing 1 lb (450 g) cooked, chopped spinach with chickpeas and adding oil and lemon juice (same quantities as in recipe) then stirring in 6 oz (175 g) plain yogurt.

Celery and cheese salad

Overall timing 10 minutes

Freezing Not suitable

To serve 4

2	Small celery hearts	2
1 oz	Walnuts	25 g
Cheese dressing		
2 oz	Blue cheese	50 g
3 tbsp	Vegetable oil	3x15 ml
1 tbsp	White wine vinegar	15 ml
	Salt and pepper	

Wash celery and leaves and drain well. Cut celery into matchsticks and put into a salad bowl. Reserve the leaves.

To make the dressing, crumble the cheese into another bowl and mix in the oil, vinegar and pepper. Taste and add a pinch of salt if necessary.

Pour dressing over celery and toss. Garnish with celery leaves and walnuts.

Coleslaw

Overall timing 20 minutes plus soaking and chilling

Freezing Not suitable

To serve 4

White cabbage	
Muscovado sugar	
Grated carrot	
Grated apple	
Sultanas	
Plain yogurt	
Mayonnaise (made with vegetable oil)	
Salt and pepper	

Quarter the cabbage and core it, then soak in iced, lightly sugared water for 30 minutes.

Drain the cabbage well and shred it. Place in a bowl with the carrot, apple and sultanas and mix together.

Make a dressing of equal parts of yogurt and mayonnaise and season to taste. Add to the cabbage mixture and fold together gently. Cover and chill for 30 minutes before serving.

Cabbage and bacon salad

Overall timing 30 minutes

Freezing Not suitable

To serve 4

4 oz	Piece of lean bacon	125 g
1¼ lb	Red and/or white cabbage	600 g
¼ teasp	Salt	1.25 ml
¼ teasp	Muscovado sugar	1.25 ml
1 tbsp	Vinegar	15 ml
2 tbsp	Plain yogurt	2 x 15 ml

Chop bacon into thick, small pieces. Cook over a medium heat in a frying pan so fat runs and bacon becomes crisp.

Meanwhile, remove core and tough outer leaves from the cabbage. Wash, then cut up and shred finely.

Place cabbage in salad bowl and sprinkle over salt and sugar. Add vinegar, then bacon and cooking fat. Toss well, spoon yogurt over and serve immediately.

Celeriac vinaigrette

Overall timing 30 minutes plus marination

Freezing Not suitable

To serve 4–6

1 lb	Celeriac	450 g
	Salt and pepper	450 g
2 tbsp	Vinegar or lemon juice	2x15 ml
Dressing		
8 tbsp	Vegetable oil	8x15 ml
3 tbsp	Wine vinegar	3x15 ml
2 teasp	Powdered mustard	2x5 ml
3	Shallots	3
3	Gherkins	3
1	Hard-boiled egg	1
1 tbsp	Chopped parsley	15 ml
	Pinch of muscovado sugar	

Peel celeriac and cut into thick slices. Cook, covered, for 15 minutes or until tender in boiling salted water to which vinegar or lemon juice has been added. Drain and put into salad bowl.

To make the dressing, beat together oil, vinegar and mustard in a bowl. Peel and finely chop shallots; finely chop gherkins and egg. Add all to dressing with chopped parsley. Add seasoning to taste and sugar.

Pour dressing over celeriac while still hot, cover and leave for 30 minutes. Taste and adjust seasoning if necessary.

Chicory salad

Overall timing 15 minutes

Freezing Not suitable

To serve 4

3	Heads of chicory	3
6 oz	Cheese	175 g
1 tbsp	Drained capers	15 ml
1 tbsp	Dijon mustard	15 ml
3 tbsp	Vegetable oil	3x15 ml
1 tbsp	Lemon juice	15 ml
	Salt and pepper	

Trim the chicory, removing any damaged outer leaves, cut off the base and remove the bitter core. Divide into leaves, wash and drain well. Shred lengthways with a stainless steel knife and put into a bowl.

Dice the cheese and add to the bowl with the capers. Mix the mustard, oil and lemon juice together with plenty of seasoning. Pour over the salad and toss lightly.

Variations

A more colourful salad with very similar texture and flavour can be made by using shredded radicchio or red chicory and bright green curly endive (a relative of chicory) if available, as well as the more common white variety. White chicory can be cut across the heads into rings instead of lengthways for a different effect. Diced or shredded cooked meat will also add a touch of colour, and extra protein if you want to serve this salad as a light lunch with bread.

Or, make an alternative dressing by mixing plain yogurt with a little tomato purée and seasoning to taste with powdered mustard, sugar, salt and pepper.

Cucumber and pepper salad

Overall timing 25 minutes plus chilling

Freezing Not suitable

To serve 4

1	Cucumber	1
1	Red pepper	1
1	Green pepper	1
8 oz	Ripe tomatoes	225 g
2	Medium onions	2
1	Garlic clove	1
4 tbsp	Vegetable oil	4x15 ml
2 tbsp	Wine vinegar	2x15 ml
$\frac{1}{2}$ teasp	Muscovado sugar	2.5 ml
$\frac{1}{2}$ teasp	Paprika	2.5 ml
	Salt and pepper	
1 tbsp	Chopped parsley	15 ml

Peel the cucumber, slice finely and put into a bowl. Wash, halve, deseed and thinly slice the peppers and add to the bowl. Wash and slice the tomatoes; peel and thinly slice the onion into rings. Add to the cucumber and pepper.

Peel and crush the garlic into a bowl. Add the oil, vinegar, sugar, paprika and seasoning and mix well with a fork. Pour over the vegetables and chill for 30 minutes.

Arrange some of the cucumber slices around the edge of a shallow serving dish. Pile the salad in the centre and sprinkle with parsley. Serve with grilled meat and boiled new potatoes or with a platter of cold meats.

Desserts

Crispy coated figs

Overall timing 1 hour

Freezing Not suitable

To serve 4

1 oz	Sultanas	25 g
2 tbsp	Rum or sherry	2x15 ml
4 oz	Plain wholemeal flour	125 g
1½ teasp	Muscovado sugar	7.5 ml
1	Whole egg	1
1 tbsp	Vegetable oil	15 ml
4 fl oz	Milk or water	120 ml
3 oz	Nibbed almonds	75 g
1 oz	Pine nuts	25 g
	Ground cinnamon	
	Ground cloves	
8 oz	Dried figs	225 g
2	Egg whites	2
	Vegetable oil for frying	

Put the sultanas in a bowl with the rum or sherry and leave to macerate for 30 minutes. Meanwhile, sift the flour and sugar into another bowl. Add the whole egg and oil and start to mix with a wooden spoon. Gradually beat in the liquid to make a smooth batter. Leave to stand.

Spread almonds on grill pan and toast till brown. Add almonds, pine nuts and a pinch each of cinnamon and cloves to the sultanas. Mix well.

Carefully slit open figs down one side. Fill with the nut and fruit mixture. Toss in a little flour, shaking off excess. Beat egg whites in a bowl till stiff. Fold into the batter mixture with a metal spoon or spatula.

Heat oil in deep-fryer to 340°F (170°C) or until a cube of stale bread browns in 1 minute. Dip figs in batter to coat, then fry in batches in the hot oil until golden all over. Remove from pan with a draining spoon and drain on kitchen paper. Serve warm.

Apricots flambé

Overall timing 20 minutes

Freezing Not suitable

To serve 4

4 oz	Muscovado sugar	125 g
1	Vanilla pod	1
$\frac{1}{4}$ pint	Water	150 ml
8	Fresh apricots	8
2 tbsp	Arrowroot or cornflour	2x15 ml
1 oz	Flaked or split almonds	25 g
4 tbsp	Orange liqueur or brandy	4x15 ml

To make the syrup, put the sugar, vanilla pod and water into a saucepan. Stir until sugar dissolves, then bring to the boil and cook over low heat, uncovered, for about 10 minutes without stirring.

Wash, dry and halve the apricots. Remove the stones and put the halves into the boiling syrup. Leave for 2 to 3 minutes to soften. Remove from heat and lift out vanilla pod, and discard it. Lift out apricots and arrange them on a warm serving plate.

Blend arrowroot or cornflour with a little water, then mix it into the syrup with a wooden spoon. Cook for 3–4 minutes over low heat, stirring continuously. Pour hot syrup over apricots and sprinkle with flaked or split almonds.

Warm the liqueur in a ladle. Set it alight and pour it over the apricots. Serve immediately.

Stewed rhubarb

Overall timing 25 minutes

Freezing Suitable

To serve 6

2 lb	Rhubarb	900 g
4–6 oz	Muscovado sugar	125–175 g
¼ pint	Water	150 ml

Wash and trim the rhubarb and cut into 1 inch (2.5 cm) lengths. Put into a saucepan with the sugar and water. Place over a moderate heat and bring to the boil, stirring gently. Cover and simmer for 5–10 minutes or till tender, shaking the pan occasionally.

Pour into a serving dish and serve hot or cold.

Variations

Add 1 lb (450 g) peeled, cored and sliced cooking apples, pears or quince, or 8 oz (225 g) topped and tailed gooseberries or redcurrants with extra sugar if required. Try flavouring plain rhubarb with 2 oz (50 g) chopped stem ginger and 2 tbsp (2x15 ml) of the syrup, or 2 teasp (2x5 ml) ground ginger. Or, tie a few elderflowers in a muslin bag and dip it into the rhubarb several times for an unusual flavour.

Carrot and raisin halva

Overall timing 1½ hours

Freezing Not suitable

To serve 4–6

12 oz	New carrots	350 g
2 pints	Milk	1.1 litres
2 inch	Piece of cinnamon stick	5 cm
½ teasp	Ground cardamom	2.5 ml
1 oz	Vegetable margarine	25 g
4 tbsp	Honey	4x15 ml
4 oz	Raisins	125 g
1 oz	Flaked almonds	25 g

Scrape and grate the carrots into a heavy-based saucepan. Add the milk and spices and bring to the boil, stirring. Simmer uncovered for about 1 hour till the milk has reduced to about ¼ pint (150 ml) and the mixture is thick.

Remove the cinnamon stick. Beat in the margarine and honey and stir in all but 1 tbsp (15 ml) of the raisins. Cook over a gentle heat for 5 minutes, stirring frequently.

Remove from the heat and stir in the almonds. Arrange on a serving dish and scatter with reserved raisins. Serve immediately or chill before serving.

Stuffed baked apples

Overall timing 30 minutes

Freezing Not suitable

To serve 6

6	Dessert apples	6
2 oz	Walnuts	50 g
2 oz	Dates	50 g
1 oz	Glacé cherries	25 g
2 oz	Muscovado sugar	50 g
4 tbsp	White wine or cider	4x15 ml
	Whipped cream (optional)	

Preheat oven to 400°F (200°C) Gas 6.

Wash apples. Remove core and a little flesh. Place apples in ovenproof dish. Chop and mix walnuts, dates and cherries. Stir in sugar. Fill apples with mixture. Pour a little wine or cider over each.

Bake for 10–15 minutes. Serve hot, with whipped cream, if liked.

Rigatoni with ricotta

Overall timing 40 minutes

Freezing Not suitable

To serve 4

8 oz	Ricotta or cottage cheese	225 g
3 tbsp	Hot water	3x15 ml
3 tbsp	Runny honey	3x15 ml
2 teasp	Ground cinnamon	2x5 ml
8 oz	Rigatoni (preferably wholemeal)	225 g
	Salt	

Put ricotta and hot water in a saucepan. Heat gently, stirring till well combined. Add the honey and cinnamon, beating well with a wooden spoon. Remove from heat and leave to cool for 20 minutes.

Meanwhile, cook the rigatoni in a large saucepan of boiling salted water till al dente. Drain and stir into the ricotta mixture. Mix well and pile into a serving dish. Serve immediately.

Fruit crumble

Overall timing 10 minutes plus cooking time

Freezing Suitable: crumble only. Bake from frozen

To serve 4-6

4 oz	Bran flakes	125 g
4 oz	Amoretti or ratafia biscuits	125 g
4 oz	Desiccated coconut	125 g
½ teasp	Grated nutmeg	2.5 ml
4 oz	Muscovado sugar	125 g
1 oz	Bran	25 g

Use a rolling pin to crush bran and biscuits roughly – they must not become powdery. Add coconut, nutmeg, sugar and bran and mix well together.

To use as a hot dessert topping, mix well with 2 oz (50 g) melted vegetable margarine and sprinkle over stewed fruit. Cook at 400°F (200°C) Gas 6 for 20 minutes. Or sprinkle over sliced fresh fruit and serve cold.

Clementines niçoise

Overall timing 15 minutes plus 2 hours maceration

Freezing Not suitable

To serve 8

8	Large clementines	8
1	Peach	1
4 oz	Cherries	125 g
8 oz	Can of pineapple rings	227 g
2 oz	Muscovado sugar	50 g
2 tbsp	Cointreau (optional)	2x15 ml
	Vanilla ice cream	

Slice the top off each clementine with a sharp knife and reserve. Scoop out the flesh with a teaspoon, taking care not to break the shell. Cover the empty shells and the tops and chill.

Cut the flesh into neat pieces, discarding the pips and pith. Peel the peach, cut in half and discard the stone. Cut into cubes. Stone the cherries, then chop flesh. Drain the pineapple and cut into pieces.

Put all the fruit into a bowl with the sugar and liqueur and leave to macerate for 2 hours.

Remove clementine shells and tops from the refrigerator. Divide the fruit and juices between the shells, add a scoop of ice cream and place the lids on top. Serve immediately in individual glass dishes.

Prunes in Madeira

Overall timing 40 minutes plus soaking and chilling

Freezing Not suitable

To serve 4

12 oz	Plump prunes	350 g
½ pint	Madeira	300 ml
½ pint	Water	300 ml
3 tbsp	Muscovado sugar	3 x 15 ml
	Strip of orange rind	
1	Cinnamon stick	1

Soak the prunes in warm water to cover for 1 hour. Drain.

Place the remaining ingredients in a saucepan and bring to the boil, stirring to dissolve the sugar. Simmer for 15 minutes.

Add the drained prunes and simmer for a further 10 minutes.

Discard the orange rind and cinnamon stick and leave to cool. Pour into a bowl, cover and chill overnight.

Rhubarb sherbet

Overall timing 1 hour

Freezing Suitable

To serve 6

1 lb	Rhubarb	450 g
4 tbsp	Water	4 x 15 ml
1 lb	Muscovado sugar	450 g
	Crushed ice cubes	

Wash and trim the rhubarb and cut into 1 inch (2.5 cm) lengths. Put into a saucepan with the water and bring to the boil. Cover and simmer for 10–15 minutes till pulpy.

Purée in a blender and rub through a sieve. Measure the syrup and make up to 1 pint (560 ml) with water if necessary. Return to the pan, add the sugar and stir over a low heat till the sugar dissolves. Increase the heat and boil without stirring till temperature reaches 220°F (115°C). Remove from the heat and leave to cool.

Just before serving, half-fill 6 sundae glasses with crushed ice cubes. Spoon the rhubarb syrup over to cover the ice and serve immediately.

Fruit in lemon jelly

Overall timing 30 minutes plus cooling and setting

Freezing Not suitable

To serve 4

1 lb	Mixed fresh fruit (pineapple, oranges, apples, pears, grapes, cherries)	450 g
2 oz	Walnuts	50 g
4 tbsp	Lemon juice	4x15 ml
3 tbsp	Muscovado sugar	3x15 ml
Jelly		
1 pint	Water	560 ml
1 tbsp	Powdered gelatine	15 ml
3 oz	Caster sugar	75 g
1	Lemon	1

Prepare the fruit and chop into neat pieces. Put into a bowl with the walnuts, lemon juice and sugar and mix well.

To make the jelly, put 4 tbsp (4x15 ml) of the water in another bowl, sprinkle gelatine over and leave till spongy. Place gelatine over pan of simmering water and add sugar. Thinly pare rind from the lemon and add to the bowl with 5 tbsp (5x15 ml) of the juice. Stir with a wooden spoon until gelatine dissolves. Add remaining water and leave for about 10 minutes to cool.

Strain cooled mixture through a doubled piece of wet muslin. If the liquid is not transparent, strain again. Leave gelatine mixture till syrupy, then stir in the fruit and nut mixture. Pour into mould. Chill in fridge for about 4 hours or until jelly is set. Turn out to serve.

Spicy fruit purée

Overall timing 1½ hours plus overnight maceration and cooling

Freezing Suitable

To serve 4

1 lb	Mixed dried fruit (figs, apricots, peaches, pears, prunes)	450 g
2 pints	Water	1.1 litres
6 oz	Muscovado sugar	175 g
2	Apples	2
2 teasp	Ground cinnamon	2x5 ml
2 tbsp	Cornflour	2x15 ml

Put the dried fruit in a large bowl with three-quarters of the water and the sugar and leave to soak overnight.

Stone the prunes. Transfer fruit to a saucepan, add remaining water and bring to the boil. Cook over a low heat for about 15 minutes.

Peel, core and slice the apples and add with cinnamon to the pan. Cook for a further 45 minutes.

Drain fruit and return liquid to the pan. Push fruit through a sieve or blend to a purée, then return to the pan.

Mix cornflour with 1 tbsp (15 ml) cold water in a bowl, then stir into fruit mixture. Bring to the boil and boil for 5 minutes, stirring, until thick. Remove from heat and allow to cool. Pour into four serving glasses and chill for 2 hours before serving.

Red and black salad

Overall timing 30 minutes plus chilling

Freezing Not suitable

To serve 4

12 oz	Prunes	350 g
2 tbsp	Muscovado sugar	2 x 15 ml
4 fl oz	Water	120 ml
4 tbsp	Orange juice	4 x 15 ml
12 oz	Strawberries	350 g
2 tbsp	Grand Marnier	2 x 15 ml

Put the prunes into a metal sieve or steamer and place over a saucepan of boiling water. Cover and steam for 15 minutes till plump.

Put the sugar and water into a saucepan and stir over a low heat till the sugar dissolves. Bring to the boil and boil without stirring for 5 minutes. Remove from the heat, stir in the orange juice and leave to cool.

Hull the strawberries. If large, cut them in half lengthways. Slit prunes and carefully remove stones. Arrange prunes and strawberries in two serving dishes.

Add the Grand Marnier to the cold syrup and spoon over the fruit. Leave to macerate in a cool place for 3–4 hours before serving.

Tropical corn cake

Overall timing 1¼ hours

Freezing Suitable: decorate after thawing

To serve 4

4 oz	Soft vegetable margarine	125 g
1¾ pints	Milk	1 litre
4 oz	Muscovado sugar	125 g
½ teasp	Vanilla essence	2.5 ml
8 oz	Fine cornmeal	225 g
3	Eggs	3
	Salt	
Decoration		
	Fresh pineapple	
9	Glacé cherries	9

Preheat the oven to 350°F (180°C) Gas 4. Use 1 oz (25 g) of the margarine to grease 9 inch (23 cm) cake tin.

Put milk, sugar and vanilla in a saucepan and bring to the boil. Stir cornmeal into milk lavishly, to prevent lumps forming. Remove pan from heat.

Separate eggs. Add egg yolks to pan, one at a time, beating well after each addition. Just melt remaining margarine and beat in.

In a bowl, beat the egg whites with a pinch of salt till soft peaks form. Carefully fold whites into cake mixture with a metal spoon. Pour mixture into tin and bake in centre of oven for about 40 minutes.

Turn cake on to wire rack to cool. Place on plate and decorate with fresh pineapple and glacé cherries.

Crumbly apple pie

Overall timing 1 hour

Freezing Suitable: reheat from frozen in 350°F (180°C) Gas 4 oven

To serve 4–6

$\frac{1}{4}$ pint	Corn oil	150 ml
3 tbsp	Cold water	3x15 ml
10 oz	Plain wholemeal flour	275 g
	Salt	
$1\frac{1}{2}$ lb	Cooking apples	700 g
4 tbsp	Muscovado sugar	4x15 ml
$\frac{1}{4}$ teasp	Ground cinnamon	1.25 ml
$\frac{1}{4}$ teasp	Grated nutmeg	1.25 ml
	Caster sugar	

Preheat oven to 400°F (200°C) Gas 6.

Mix together corn oil and water in a bowl. Sift in flour and pinch of salt, then mix with a fork to a soft dough. A little extra flour may be needed to make it less sticky and easier to roll out.

Roll out two-thirds of pastry between 2 sheets of greaseproof paper and use to line 8 inch (20 cm) pie dish. Prick with fork.

Peel, core and slice apples. Fill pastry case with sliced apples and sprinkle with sugar and spices.

Roll out remaining pastry to a circle large enough to cover apples. Dampen pastry edges with water, then place lid on top, pinching edges of pastry together to seal. Bake in oven for about 25 minutes till golden. Serve warm or cold, sprinkled with caster sugar.

Variation

Add more flavour and fibre to pie by mixing apples with blackberries and adding bran to pastry. Or substitute other fruits such as red or black currants, gooseberries or rhubarb. By adding about 2 teasp (2x5 ml) cornflour to the sugar and tossing fruit in this before placing on pastry, the juices thicken during cooking instead of soaking into the pastry.

Peanut pie

Overall timing 1¼ hours

Freezing Not suitable

To serve 6–8

Pastry		
4 oz	Self-raising wholemeal flour	125 g
½ teasp	Salt	2.5 ml
2 tbsp	Muscovado sugar	2x15 ml
2 oz	Vegetable margarine	50 g
1	Egg yolk	1
2 tbsp	Milk	2x15 ml
Filling		
4 oz	Roasted unsalted peanuts	125 g
1	Egg	1
3 oz	Muscovado sugar	75 g
4 oz	Golden syrup	125 g
½ teasp	Vanilla essence	2.5 ml

Preheat the oven to 350°F (180°C) Gas 4.

To make pastry, sift flour, salt and sugar into a bowl. Rub in the margarine. Add egg yolk and gradually mix in enough milk to bind to a soft dough. Roll out dough and use to line an 8 inch (20 cm) fluted flan ring.

To make filling, preheat the grill. Remove the shells from the peanuts. Place nuts on a baking tray and grill them for 2 minutes, shaking the tray so they brown lightly all over. Remove and allow to cool.

Whisk the egg and sugar in a bowl till light and frothy. Add syrup and continue to beat till thick. Stir in the peanuts and vanilla essence.

Pour the peanut mixture into the flan ring and bake for 30 minutes. Cover with foil and bake for a further 5–10 minutes. Lift off the foil, leave the pie till almost cool, then remove from tin.

Nutty honey cake

Overall timing 1 hour

Freezing Not suitable

To serve 8–10

6 oz	Vegetable margarine	175 g
3 oz	Clear honey	75 g
5 oz	Plain flour	150 g
5 oz	Plain wholemeal flour	150 g
Filling		
4 oz	Mixed nuts	125 g
2 oz	Sultanas	50 g
1 teasp	Ground cinnamon	5 ml
	Clear honey	

Preheat the oven to 350°F (180°C) Gas 4.

Cream margarine with honey till light and fluffy. Mix in sifted flours to make a dough. Roll out half dough on a floured surface and press into greased and lined 7 inch (18 cm) round tin.

Chop nuts and mix with sultanas and cinnamon. Bind with honey. Spread filling over dough in tin.

Roll out remaining dough and cover filling. Press edges to seal. Bake for 30–40 minutes till golden. Cool in the tin.

Sweet sesame biscuits

Overall timing 30–40 minutes

Freezing Not suitable

Makes 20

3 oz	Vegetable margarine	75 g
4 oz	Demerara sugar	100 g
1	Small egg	1
6 oz	Self-raising wholemeal flour	175 g
2 tbsp	Sesame seeds	2 x 15 ml
	Vanilla essence	

Preheat the oven to 375°F (190°C) Gas 5.

Beat the margarine with the sugar until light and fluffy. Beat in the egg. Sift in the flour. Add 1 tbsp (15 ml) of the sesame seeds and a few drops of vanilla essence. Mix to a stiff dough.

Shape the dough into small balls and place on greased baking trays. Flatten the tops slightly with a fork and sprinkle with the remaining sesame seeds.

Bake in the centre of the oven for 15–20 minutes. Cool on a wire rack.

Treacle and nut slices

Overall timing 2 hours

Freezing Not suitable

Makes 24

5 oz	Plain wholemeal flour	150 g
10 oz	Demerara sugar	275 g
5 tbsp	Vegetable oil	5x15 ml
12 oz	Chopped nuts	350 g
6 oz	Fresh wholemeal breadcrumbs	175 g
	Grated rind of 1 orange	
1	Large cooking apple	1
2	Eggs	2
6 oz	Treacle	175 g

Sift flour into a bowl, add 2 oz (50 g) sugar and oil and mix well to make a soft dough. Chill.

Meanwhile, mix nuts with remaining sugar, breadcrumbs and orange rind. Peel and quarter the apple and grate into mixture. Add eggs and treacle and mix well.

Preheat the oven to 350°F (180°C) Gas 4. Divide the dough into 3 equal portions. Roll out each piece thinly to a rectangle the same size as 12x9 inch (30x23 cm) baking tin. Place 1 rectangle in bottom of tin, spread half filling over and smooth top. Cover with another piece of dough, spread remaining filling over and lightly press on remaining dough.

Bake in the centre of the oven for 1 hour till a skewer inserted in centre comes out clean. Cool, then cut lengthways into 4 strips and diagonally across the strips to make diamond shapes. Sift icing sugar over, if liked.

Almond biscuits

Overall timing 40 minutes plus standing

Freezing Not suitable

Makes about 30

2	Eggs	2
4 oz	Light brown sugar	100 g
½ teasp	Vanilla essence	2.5 ml
4 oz	Self-raising wholemeal flour	100 g
2 oz	Flaked almonds	50 g

Whisk the eggs until frothy, then gradually whisk in the sugar. Add the vanilla essence and sifted flour and whisk for 3 minutes. Fold in the almonds.

Drop spoonfuls of the mixture on to foil-lined baking trays, spreading them into ovals about 1 inch (2.5 cm) wide. Leave to stand for 1 hour.

Preheat the oven to 325°F (170°C) Gas 3.

Bake the biscuits in the centre of the oven for about 15 minutes or till puffed. Allow to cool slightly on the tray, then remove to a wire rack to cool completely.

Crunchy cookies

Overall timing 25 minutes

Freezing Suitable

Makes 24

5 oz	All-Bran	150 g
2 oz	Desiccated coconut	50 g
3 oz	Sultanas	75 g
2 tbsp	Golden syrup	2x15 ml
7 fl oz	Can of condensed milk	200 ml

Preheat the oven to 375°F (190°C) Gas 5.

In a bowl mix together bran, coconut and sultanas. Stir the syrup into the condensed milk, then stir the mixture into other ingredients to make a fairly stiff consistency.

Place large spoonfuls of the mixture at well-spaced intervals on greased baking trays. Bake in two batches if necessary, towards top of oven for 15 minutes. Lift biscuits on to wire rack to cool.

All-bran loaf

Overall timing 2½ hours

Freezing Suitable

Makes 1 loaf

2 oz	All-Bran	50 g
5 oz	Muscovado sugar	150 g
4 oz	Chopped dates or dried fruit	125 g
8 fl oz	Milk	220 ml
	Pinch of salt	
1 teasp	Allspice	5 ml
6 oz	Plain wholemeal flour	175 g
1½ teasp	Baking powder	7.5 ml
2 oz	Vegetable margarine	50 g

In a bowl mix together bran, sugar, fruit, milk and salt and leave to soak for 1 hour.

Preheat oven to 375°F (190°C) Gas 5. Sift allspice, flour and baking powder together, then mix into fruit with melted margarine. Beat well. Place in greased 1 lb (450 g) loaf tin. Bake for 1 hour in centre of oven. Turn out on to wire rack to cool. When cold, serve sliced and buttered. Ice, if liked.

Date squares

Overall timing 1 hour

Freezing Suitable

Makes 12

1 lb	Stoned dates	450 g
3 tbsp	Water	3x15 ml
1 tbsp	Lemon juice	15 ml
7 oz	Self-raising wholemeal flour	200 g
1 oz	Bran	25 g
4 oz	Vegetable margarine	125 g
3 oz	Muscovado sugar	75 g
1	Egg	1
1 tbsp	Milk	15 ml

Preheat the oven to 350°F (180°C) Gas 4.

Chop dates and place in saucepan with water and lemon juice. Cook, stirring, till mixture is like a paste – about 5 minutes. Leave to cool.

Place flour and bran in mixing bowl. Rub in margarine till mixture resembles bread-crumbs. Add 2 oz (50 g) of the sugar. Separate egg. Add yolk and milk to dough and knead till smooth.

Divide dough in half. Press one half over bottom of greased 9 inch (23 cm) square cake tin. Spread with date mixture. Roll out rest of dough and place on dates.

Lightly whisk egg white with a fork. Brush over top and sprinkle with remaining caster sugar. Bake for 30–35 minutes. Cut into squares while hot and leave in tin to cool before serving.

Swiss fruit bread

Overall timing 40 minutes plus rising

Freezing Suitable

Makes 3 small loaves

1 lb	Strong wholemeal flour	450 g
4 teasp	Dried yeast	4x5 ml
2 oz	Muscovado sugar	50 g
½ pint	Lukewarm milk	300 ml
2 oz	Melted vegetable margarine	50 g
1	Egg	1
4 oz	Sultanas	125 g
2 oz	Candied peel	50 g
1 oz	Wheat germ	25 g
	Grated rind of 1 lemon	
½ teasp	Salt	2.5 ml
1	Egg white	1

Sift 4 oz (100 g) of the flour into a large mixing bowl. Add yeast, 1 teasp (5 ml) sugar and the milk and mix to a smooth batter. Leave in a warm place for 15–20 minutes until frothy.

Stir margarine and beaten egg into yeast mixture. Add sultanas, peel, wheat germ, lemon rind and remaining sugar and sift in remaining flour and salt. Mix to a soft dough. Knead until smooth and elastic. Cover and leave in a warm place to rise till doubled in size.

Tip dough on to a floured surface and knead again till smooth. Divide dough into 3 pieces and knead each into a smooth ball. Place in greased loaf tins, cover and leave to rise again till doubled in size.

Preheat the oven to 400°F (200°C) Gas 6. Lightly beat egg white and brush over loaves. Bake in the centre of the oven for about 35 minutes, changing shelf position after 20 minutes to prevent uneven cooking. Cool in tins for a few minutes, then turn on to a wire rack to cool.

Peanut brittle

Overall timing 40 minutes

Freezing Not suitable

Makes about 1 lb (450 g)

10 oz	Monkey nuts	275 g
8 oz	Muscovado sugar	225 g
2 tbsp	Water	2x15 ml

Preheat oven to 425°F (220°C) Gas 7. Place shelled halved nuts on baking tray and bake for 5 minutes to dry – the nuts must not brown.

Put sugar and water in pan and stir till sugar dissolves. Boil steadily without stirring till rich golden brown. Remove from heat and lightly stir in nuts with oiled handle of wooden spoon.

Pour on to oiled tray or marble slab and spread to even thickness. Mark top into squares. Leave to set before breaking up.

Fruity barley delights

Overall timing 40 minutes

Freezing Not suitable

Makes about 24

4 oz	Pearl barley	125 g
1	Orange	1
8 oz	Dried apricots	225 g
1 tbsp	Orange flower water	15 ml
4 oz	Cottage cheese	125 g
4 tbsp	Ground almonds	4x15 ml
Coating		
2 oz	Sesame seeds	50 g
2 tbsp	Caster sugar	2x15 ml
1 teasp	Allspice	5 ml

Cover pearl barley with water. Bring to the boil and cook for 30 minutes or till barely tender.

Meanwhile, peel orange and cut into quarters. Remove pips and put flesh through the mincer along with the dried apricots. Add orange flower water, cottage cheese (squeezed dry in muslin) and ground almonds. Mix well.

When barley is cooked, drain well then return to pan and allow to steam dry for several minutes, stirring gently. Leave to cool, then add to other ingredients. Knead well with fingers to give an even consistency.

Form into about 24 small balls about 1 inch (2.5 cm) diameter. Mix together sesame seeds, sugar and allspice on a plate. Roll balls in mixture till coated all over. Place in fridge till well chilled.

Glazed stuffed sweetmeats

Overall timing 45 minutes plus cooling

Freezing Not suitable

To serve 8–10

6 oz	Dates	175 g
	Marzipan or almond paste	
6 oz	Prunes	175 g
6 oz	Walnut halves	175 g
12 oz	Light brown sugar	350 g
½ pint	Water	300 ml
	Cream of tartar	

Slit open the dates and remove the stones. Fill with a small piece of marzipan or almond paste. Fill the prunes in the same way. Sandwich together pairs of walnut halves with marzipan or almond paste.

Place the sugar, water and a pinch of cream of tartar in a saucepan and bring to the boil, stirring to dissolve the sugar. Boil until the syrup reaches the thread stage (a little cooled and pulled between the fingers will form a crunchy thread). Remove the pan from the heat and dip the base into cold water to stop the syrup cooking further.

Using a slotted spoon, dip the stuffed fruits and nuts into the syrup to coat on all sides. Arrange on an oiled wire rack, not touching each other, and allow to cool and set.

Fruits in succulent caramel

Overall timing 30 minutes

Freezing Not suitable

Makes 52

4	Prunes	4
2	Very firm peaches	2
4	Apricots	4
12	Large white grapes	12
12	Firm cherries	12
4	Walnuts	4
4	Dates	4
9 oz	Granulated sugar	250 g
4 fl oz	Water	120 ml
1 tbsp	Glucose or runny honey	15 ml

Choose fruit in prime condition. Prunes should be covered in boiling water and left to soak for 2 hours before removing stones. Cut the peaches into 4 and halve apricots, removing stones. Dry well. Shell the walnuts and stone dates.

Put the sugar and water in a saucepan. Add the glucose or honey and place over high heat until it colours, stirring all the time with a wooden spoon. Remove pan from heat and place over hot water.

Drop some of the fruits into the caramel, turning them carefully with a wooden spoon till coated. Lift out the fruit with a skewer and place on oiled marble or baking tray, making sure they don't touch each other. Coat remaining fruit with caramel. If caramel begins to harden in pan before all the fruit has been coated, place the pan over gently boiling water before continuing.

Insert a cocktail stick into each fruit and leave to go completely cold before arranging on serving dish.

Popcorn balls

Overall timing 40 minutes

Freezing Not suitable

Makes about 20

2 tbsp	Corn oil	2x15 ml
3½ oz	Popping corn	100 g
2 oz	Vegetable margarine	50 g
6 oz	Golden syrup	175 g
2 oz	Caster sugar	50 g

Heat the oil in a large heavy-based saucepan. Add the corn, put on the lid and shake the pan over a medium heat till the corn begins to pop. Continue shaking the pan till all the corn has popped.

Crush the popcorn on a board with a rolling pin till quite fine.

Put the margarine, syrup and sugar into a saucepan and stir over a gentle heat till the sugar dissolves. Bring to the boil, cover and cook for 3 minutes so that any sugar crystals on the sides of the pan dissolve in the steam.

Uncover and boil steadily to a temperature of 238°F (115°C) or till a little of the mixture dropped into cold water forms a soft ball.

Remove from the heat and stir in three-quarters of the popcorn. Leave aside till cool enough to handle, then shape the mixture into 1½ inch (4cm) diameter balls and roll in the remaining popcorn till evenly coated. Leave to set.

Cottage stuffed prunes

Overall timing 50 minutes plus soaking

Freezing Not suitable

Makes 16

16	Large plump prunes	16
4 oz	Cottage cheese	125 g
2 teasp	Milk	2x5 ml
	Grated rind of ½ orange	
2 tbsp	Honey	2x15 ml
1 oz	Roasted salted peanuts	25 g

Put the prunes into a bowl, cover with warm water and soak for 1 hour. Tip the prunes and soaking liquid into a saucepan, cover and simmer for 10 minutes till tender. Drain and leave to cool.

Cut the prunes across lengthways and carefully remove stones.

Press the cottage cheese through a sieve into a bowl. Beat in the milk, orange rind and honey. Finely chop the peanuts and add half to the cheese. Mix well. Pipe or spoon the mixture into the prunes so the stuffing shows slightly. Sprinkle with the remaining peanuts. Arrange on lettuce leaves in serving dish.

Index